Learning Adventures:
Basic Math

Cindy Koepp

Lumen Anime
Citron Concassé
Aberdeen, Washington, USA

Learning Adventures: Basic Math

© Copyright 2022 by Cindy Koepp

All Rights Reserved, Published in the United States by Lumen Anime, an imprint of Citron Concassé. No part of this book may be reproduced or transmitted in any form or by any means, electronic or mechanical, including photocopying, recording, or by information storage and retrieval systems without written permission of the Publisher with exceptions as to brief quotes, references, articles, reviews, and certain other noncommercial uses permitted by copyright law.

For permissions and queries, contact the publisher at:
info@citronconcasse.com

PRINTING HISTORY
First Edition
May 2022

ISBN-10: 0999592779
ISBN-13: 978-0-9995927-7-9

CREDITS
Cover Art by: Kylie Jude of Frozen Creek Studios

PUBLISHER'S NOTE

This series was written by a teacher for teachers and parents in need of teaching aids to support learning in the language arts and mathematics. Copies of this work or any part of it, may be made for the explicit intent to use within an educational setting.

What's This Book About Anyway?

For 14 years, I taught elementary, mostly in fourth grade. During that time, I made up over 500 word problems to use in my class.

This book contains 170 problems I've used with 4th and 5th graders to cover basic number sense, multiplication, addition, division, subtraction, fractions, decimals, and estimation. The problems cover a range of difficulty, and I've included suggestions for ways to simplify or complicate the problems in the Answer Key.

Other titles in the Learning Adventures Series include:

Mathematics: Geometry and Measurement

Mathematics: Advanced Concepts (Mathematics)

Language Arts: Grammar

Language Arts: Reading, Spelling, Writing Process, and Cursive

Writing

Projects

Table of Contents

Number Sense: Problems 1-17	1
Basic Four-Functions: Problems 18-120	7
Decimals: Problems 121-144	59
Estimations, Range: Problems 145-161	71
Fractions: Problems 162-170	81
Answer Key with solving strategies and suggested modifications	85

Number Sense

1. On vacation, Bob traveled six hundred sixty-eight miles. Fred traveled five hundred fifteen miles. Skippy traveled four hundred ninety-one miles. George traveled six hundred eighty-four miles. Arrange the names from least to greatest distance traveled.

2. Lenny Monade owned a lemonade stand. On Saturday, he had one hundred eighty-four customers. On Friday, he had one hundred twenty-eight customers. On Monday, he had ninety-eight customers. On Wednesday, he had one hundred twelve customers. Order the days from the busiest to the slowest.

Basic Math

3. What is the largest 4-digit number you can make without repeating digits or using consecutive digits anywhere in the number (adjacent or not)?

4. What is the smallest 4-digit number you can make without repeating digits or using consecutive digits anywhere in the number (adjacent or not)? No, you can't start with 0.

5. What is the largest 4-digit number you can make?

6. What is the smallest 4-digit number you can make? No, you can't start with 0.

7. The way this number is written has major issues with the place values. Fix the problem. (HINT: Write out each part and then combine the place values that overlap so it reads right).

Seventeen thousand, twelve hundred four

8. Write four different 9-digit numbers that all have a 5 in the ten thousands place, a 7 in the hundreds place, and a 4 in the millions place. No repeating digits allowed in the same number. Now put the numbers in order from greatest to least.

9. Which number is greater?
Seventy-two million, nine hundred four thousand, seven and two hundredths

Or

Seventy-two million, nine hundred forty thousand, seven and two hundredths

10. Penny Sill has five pens and twelve pencils. Write the fact family for the number of writing implements Penny has.

Basic Math

11. What is the smallest 4-digit number you can make without repeating digits or using consecutive digits? No, you can't start with 0.

12. What is the largest 4-digit number you can make without repeating digits or using consecutive digits?

13. What numbers between 1 and 20 are prime?

14. What numbers between 1 and 25 have two or three for a factor?

15. Find all the factors of 256.

16. If the prefix "mill-" means 1000, why are "millions" located where they are in a number?

17. Why can't I have a place value occupied by a double-digit number (like 13 or 27)?

Basic Math

Basic Four-Functions

18. Willy Quit likes to play his guitar for hours at a time. He played his guitar for five hours on Monday, six hours on Tuesday, Eight hours on Wednesday, two hours on Thursday, and ten hours on Friday. How many hours did he play his guitar that week?

19. R.U. Done-Yet ran fifteen miles every day for one week. How many miles did he run?

Basic Math

20. Won Togo is stuffing his face with candy. He started with fifty-two pieces of candy and ate thirteen of them before Mom caught him. How many pieces are left?

21. Miya Frend picked up a new species of snake. This weirdo has all his scales in stripes. Each stripe has sixty scales. If there are thirty-two stripes, how many total scales are there?

22. Cookie Teal has a strange new kind of bird. This bird has five colors of feathers. Each color has ninety-two feathers. How many feathers are there altogether?

23. Zane Neepal picked up a new species of snake. This weirdo has all his scales in stripes. Each stripe has six scales. If there are ninety scales, how many total stripes are there?

Basic Math

24. Bert Tee has a strange new kind of bird. This bird has five colors of feathers. Each color has the same number of feathers. If there are one hundred twenty-five feathers altogether, how many of each color are there?

25. Jo Ger ran twelve miles. The next day, Jo ran twice as far. How many miles did Jo run in two days?

26. Mina Byrd's parrot ate fifty-eight pellets. The next day, he ate three times as much. How many pellets did he eat in two days?

27. Misty Rios is trying out for a part in the school play. If she gets the part she's hoping for, she'll have to memorize seventy-two lines. One of the other parts in the play has one hundred forty-four lines. The play is in eight weeks. How many lines must she memorize each week to be ready on time?

Basic Math

28. A certain forest covered fifty-eight thousand, four hundred seventy-five acres. Trees For You came out and added another seventeen thousand fourteen acres of seedlings around the outside. When the trees grow up, how many acres will the forest cover? Write the answer in numbers and in words.

29. T-shirts cost nine dollars each. Lena Onme wants to buy ten T-shirts. If Lena has one hundred dollars in her pocket, can Lena buy the T-shirts?

30. Rocky Cliff dug up seven hundred thousand pebbles. Billy Gote dug up thirty-five thousand, two hundred six pebbles. They each put half their pebbles in a bucket. How many pebbles are in the bucket?

31. Joe Kerr had seven hundred sixteen matchbox cars. For his birthday, his aunt gave him one half as many. How much does Joe have now?

Basic Math

32. Mary Bell had four thousand, eighty-two marbles. She purchased two hundred seventy more at one store and sold one thousand six hundred five at a garage sale. Write how many she has now in words.

33. Maya Cann saved sixty-eight cans for recycling. Uri Cann saved four times as many as Maya did. How many cans do they have altogether?

34. The gravity on the moon is 1/6 of that on Earth. Astro Knott weighs 105 pounds on Earth. What would Astro weigh on the moon?

35. Wheelan Axel really likes to write. One story he wrote was 120,000 words long. No kidding. If he can write 200 words on a page, how many pages long was it?

Basic Math

36. Hattie Molly eats jalapeños faster than anyone. If she can eat a jalapeno in 35 seconds, how long did it take her to eat 25 jalapenos?

37. Sally Kritter has a crazy little bird. She makes spitballs at the rate of 5 per minute. If she did that for 1 hour, how many spitballs would she make?

38. What is the sum of the first 20 even numbers (starting with 0)?

39. Mike Arr loves to write stories. Every night after finishing his homework, Mike works on his latest novel, Running Tally, which is about a girl nicknamed Tally who solves crimes by chasing down the bad guys. The average novel is 90,000 words. If Mike finishes his novel in 300 days, how many words did he write each day?

Basic Math

40. Dot Maytricks is having problems with her printer. Every time she sends a file to be printed, the printer shoots out an extra page with random spots on it. She discovered this problem at the end of the day. If she had printed sixteen files that day and each file was a page long, how many pages came out of the printer?

41. Al LeGator has a type of lizard called a caiman. Al's lizard eats one chicken drumstick every day. Drumsticks come in packages of ten. How many packages does Al have to buy to keep his caiman fed for the month of October?

42. In 2014, Ella Jibble wants to be a member of a band, but she has to be at least fourteen years old. She was born two years after her brother, who was born in 1999. Is Ella old enough in 2014?

43. Steve needs to collect forty-five cans for a recycling project. Each person on his block gives him four cans. If there are fifteen people on his block, did he reach his goal?

Basic Math

44. Kit T. Littur hates cleaning up after her cat, Lunchmeat. Kit wants to hire her little brother to do it. If Kit makes $10 babysitting every night and needs $20 a week for herself, what is the maximum she could offer her brother to clean up after Lunchmeat every week?

45. Kat Agorey is a player in a game show. She has to pick from one of five categories of questions. Each category has six questions. Each question has four possible answer choices. How many total answer choices are there?

46. Alexus is running a lemonade stand. Her goal is to make $10. She made enough lemonade for 25 cups. If she sells it all, what will she have to charge to make her goal?

47. Connie Book has 100 comic books. Each comic book has 72 pages. How many total pages are in the comic books?

Basic Math

48. Ted E. Behr has 750 tiny teddy bears. Each one is less than 2" tall. His dad made him a special cabinet to keep them all in. Since he started his tiny teddy bear collection, Ted has received 2 bears every week. For how many weeks has he been collecting tiny teddy bears?

49. Reid Bukes reads one chapter in a book every day. Each chapter has about 1000 words in it. If the book has 14 chapters, how many words are there?

50. Grey Nola eats 5 granola bars for a snack at school every day. He's in school every day for 200 days. How many total granola bars does he eat?

51. Miss Understand wants to divide her students into groups of 4 each for a project. There are 8 boys and 14 girls in the class. How many groups will there be? If there are unassigned students, what does she do with them?

Basic Math

52. Miles Togo is going skiing. He buys five bottles of water for the day. He spent a total of $22 for the water. How much did each bottle of water cost?

53. Alexus has two hundred six pieces of cake. She planned to have enough for each guest at the party to have four pieces of cake. How many guests is she expecting?

54. Tyya has sixty-two bird feathers. She needs four for an art project. How many of those projects can she do? If she has leftovers, what should she do with them?

55. Penny Pensill has five boxes of green pens and two boxes of black pens. Each box, regardless of color, contains twenty-four pens. How many total pens does she have?

Basic Math

56. Penny Ferthots has thirty-three fuzzy pencil cushions. She's tired of them and wants to get rid of them by splitting them evenly among her four friends. How many does each friend get? If there are extras, what does Penny do with them?

57. Kameron has a collection of baseball caps. Each cap has a logo made with 2000 stitches. There are 2,634,000 stitches in his baseball cap collection. How many baseball caps does he have?

58. Herb Plant wrote the following expanded number on his paper: 30000+200+3. What is that number divided by 4?

59. Perry Yitt has twelve toys for big parrots in his house. Each one costs about twenty dollars. He also has five toys for small parrots in his house. Each one costs about fifteen dollars. How much did he spend for all his parrot toys?

Basic Math

60. There are one hundred seventeen kids and ten adults going on a field trip. One bus can hold fifty people, not counting the bus driver. How many buses will be needed?

61. There are eighty-five elephants and twelve zebras in a parade. If each zebra has twenty-eight black stripes, how many ears are in the parade?

62. Mr. E. Meet has 133 pencils. His class has twenty kids. How many pencils will each kid get if everyone gets the same amount?

63. Ima Nutt asked her mom and dad for pieces of ribbon for her friends. Each parent gave her twelve pieces of ribbon. If she has six friends and they all get the same number of pieces, how many ribbons will each friend get?

Basic Math

64. Rex Cars loves kumquats. The first time he went to the store, he bought 18 kumquats. The second time, he bought 17. He bought none the third time but picked up a lovely bunch of 58 coconuts. How many kumquats did Rex get altogether?

65. Ima Loon likes to play football. On Monday, she caught 106 passes. On Tuesday, she caught 48 fewer passes. On Wednesday she caught 93 passes, and on Thursday she caught a third as many as she did on Wednesday. What is the difference between the total number of passes caught on Monday and Wednesday and the total number of passes caught on Tuesday and Thursday?

66. Candy Kane has 247 candies that she wants to distribute equally to her nieces and nephews but only if they come to her house to help her with a project. She has a total of 6 nieces and nephews, but she has no idea how many will come help. Fill in a chart to show the number of candies her nieces and nephews will get if they come over.

67. You're helping a little kid with homework. He needs to multiply 84x37, but he doesn't know how. Explain one way to do it without looking up the answer in a table or chart.

Basic Math

68. Rhode Island is the smallest state in the United States. Twice the area is two thousand, four hundred eight square miles. Write the area of Rhode Island in words.

69. Brett Less ran 8 miles. It took him 2 hours. If he ran the same speed the whole way, how far did he run in 60 minutes?

70. X. Sample has eight dogs. Her unfortunate dogs have fleas. If each dog had the same number of fleas, how many fleas were there on each dog if there were two hundred fifty-six total fleas?

71. Write today's date. Remove the punctuation. Divide by 15.

Basic Math

72. Moe Zart sees 5 little stars twinkle-twinkling in the sky in what appears to be a 3 square-inch area. If Moe can see a 15 square inch area, how many little stars does Moe see twinkle-twinkling in all?

73. Perry Itt has a bird named Fuzzball. Fuzzball is molting or shedding feathers. She's shedding 1 feather every two days. She grows in 7 feathers a week. Will she lose all her feathers?

74. Chip R. Chirper has a bird named Mouthy. Mouthy practiced his vocabulary by running through his entire library of sound effects and words. He didn't repeat anything. If he practiced for an hour and a half and managed one word or sound effect every two seconds, how many words and sound effects does he know?

75. The low and the high temperatures in one day were both odd numbers. Does that mean that the change in temperature was an even number or an odd number? Prove it.

Basic Math

76. Bo Urd does bizarre things like perforate paper. He can make 43 holes per minute. How many minutes will it take for him to make at least 623 holes?

77. Dewey Kair has eighty-four thousand bottle caps in his collection. Every year, he collected twelve thousand new ones. If Dewey is fifteen years old now, when did he start collecting?

78. Bob Tale keeps rabbits. He has five mini rabbits, ten lop-eared rabbits, and six long-haired rabbits. How many total rabbit feet are in his rabbit pens?

79. Allie Katt has a whole bunch of cats in her house. She has one poor, little tabby she rescued from the pound. This tabby had been in a fight, and he'd lost an ear. Of her other cats, six of them are orange, four of them are gray, two of them are black, and one of them is white. How many total cat ears are in the house?

Basic Math

80. Kitty Katt went into business walking cats around the neighborhood. She has fifty regular customers. Forty of them are short-haired cats. The rest are long-haired. If she makes an average of $1000.00 every month, how much does she charge for cat-walking?

81. Kat Toiz has a very finicky cat named Phydeaux. Phydeaux will only play with one kind of toy, and he tends to destroy it every four days. The toy costs $5. If Kat can make $10 per week by cleaning up the kitchen every night, can she make enough to keep Phydeaux supplied with his favorite toy?

82. Mai Dawg's poodle has fleas. Mai needs to go get some flea soap, but she can't afford a whole lot. She finds a 4 oz bottle for $5 and an 8 oz bottle for $7. Which is a better buy?

83. A new shop called Puppy Love has opened up for people who want to play with puppies without taking them home. For the cost of $10 per hour, you can play with a puppy by yourself. The shop has 15 puppies right now. What is the maximum amount of money they can make in one 8-hour day?

Basic Math

84. Jewel Ree has five bracelets. She has a kit that allows her to make ten times that many. How many will she have when she's finished making bracelets?

85. Bob L. Hedd is collecting bobble head pets. He found a bunch on sale at Wally World for $2 each. For his birthday, he got $5 from each of 6 relatives. If he spends all his birthday money on bobble head pets, how many will he be able to get?

86. Every year his birds molt. Moe Ult gets 58 feathers from Dot and 82 feathers from Huey. After 4 years, how many feathers does Moe have from those two?

87. Penny Earned has written eight novels. Each one is about ninety-thousand words long. She has also written one hundred seventy-two stories. The length varies, but the average length is about thirty-thousand words. How many total words has she written in her novels and stories?

Basic Math

88. There are one hundred sixty adult novels and seventy-two kid novels in some boxes. The average adult novel is about three hundred pages long. The average kid novel is one hundred fifty pages long. About how many pages of novels are in the boxes?

89. Jewel Urr is making a bunch of jewelry for herself and seven of her favorite friends. Each person gets a necklace made of fifteen blue beads, five red beads, and seventy green beads. Each person also gets a bracelet made of six blue beads, one red bead, and fourteen green beads. How many total beads will she need?

90. Harry Dawg takes 58 seconds to do his hair in the morning. Bea Quick takes 10 times as long as Harry to do her hair. How many minutes does it take Bea to do her hair in the morning?

91. Annie Versary and Bert Day are going head to head in Around the World. Annie can answer one multiplication problem every two seconds. Bert can answer thirty-one problems in one minute. Who is most likely to win the round?

Basic Math

92. Martina, a gray and yellow cockatiel, likes to wear her bell for a hat. Each time she does, she wears her hat for 5 minutes. On Monday, she does that 4 times. On Tuesday, she does that 19 times. On Wednesday, she does that 83 times. On Thursday, she does that 13 times. On Friday, she goes all out and does that 90 times. How many minutes every week does she spend wearing her bell like a hat?

93. Rex Cars must make multiplication flashcards, but he doesn't want to make more than he absolutely has to. He decided to eliminate ones that are duplicates because they're in the same fact family. If he does only one in a fact family, how many does he have to do? (use numerals 1-12)

94. Rose Bush has to make addition flashcards, but she doesn't want to make more than she absolutely has to. She decided to eliminate ones that are duplicates because they're in the same fact family. If she does only one in a fact family, how many does she have to do? (use numerals 1-10)

95. Jan bought 7 pies and 4 cakes. The pies cost $8 each. The cakes cost half as much. How much change will Jan get back from a $100 bill?

Basic Math

96. In 1870 the population of Texas was 818,579. If the population grew by 2,000 every year since 1870, what is the population now? Write the new population in words.

97. Someone donated the weirdest dogs to a local fire station. They were all dalmatians, and although they weren't identical, they all had the same number of spots. Altogether, there were eighteen large spots, twenty-seven medium-sized spots, and fifty-four small spots. If there are three dogs, how many spots are on each dog?

98. Shaw Perr bought 5 ties and 4 shirts for his dad. Each shirt cost $15. The total cost for all the shirts and ties was $100. How much did each tie cost?

99. Kay Bull is going to get cable internet for Christmas. If the set up charge is $99 and the cost per month is $35, what will be the cost for the first year of cable internet?

Basic Math

100. Mike Ees's dachshund sleeps a lot. She sleeps for two minutes out of every five in the day. How many hours does Mike's dog sleep in one day?

101. Peter Piper picks pecks of pickled peppers. If Peter Piper picks seven pecks of pickled peppers every day, how many pecks of pickled peppers will Peter Piper pick in the month of September? (He does not get days off.)

102. If a canner can can cans, I suspect that a canner can can cans at the rate of ten cans per hour. If I employ a canner to can cans for three eight-hour days, how many cans can a canner can if a canner can can cans?

103. What is the product of the first 4 prime numbers?

Basic Math

104. Kanya Seeyit does jumping jacks every day during recess. She can do 30 jumping jacks per minute. Recess is 30 minutes long. How many jumping jacks does Kanya do in one week?

105. Dee Side and Mai Sandmen are having a contest to see who can collect the most bird stamps in one year. Dee buys 5 stamps every week with his allowance. For Dee's birthday, he received 26 bird stamps from his grandma. Mai's dad works in a store that sells old stamps. He brings her one new bird stamp every day. At the end of the year, who wins by how much?

106. Jim Nasium is starting a new exercise program. His doctor recommended he get a minimum of one hundred fifty minutes of exercise every week. He signed up for a program that lets him work out at the gym for thirty-five minutes a day, four days a week. Will he meet the goal his doctor set?

107. Harry Beast has eight dogs. Each dog eats ten pounds of dog food every week. How much food will Harry need to feed his dogs for one year?

Basic Math

108. P. Yourblud has heard about a new breed of dog called a Canardly. He simply must get one for his dog collection. Canardlies cost $2000. If Mr. Yourblud can save $15 per week, how many days before he can get his Canardly?

109. To make a large gourd shaker, Gordon Mihand needs seventy-two shells. To make a small gourd shaker, he needs half as many shells as the large gourd shaker. He needs to make two large gourd shakers and three small gourd shakers. How many shells will he need altogether?

110. Jim Nasium drives 30 miles to work every morning. On Monday evenings, he drives the same distance home. On Tuesdays, he needs to drive an additional 5 miles to go to the store. On Wednesdays and Thursdays, he goes an additional 16 miles to pick up his friend from work. On Fridays, he takes a different route home to avoid traffic. That route is 38 miles long. In 5 days, how many total miles does he drive?

111. Susie sells seashells by the seashore. If Susie sells seventy seashells by the seashore every Sunday afternoon for sixty-seven weeks, how many seashells does Susie sell by the seashore?

Basic Math

112. Priddy Messay has eight dresses. Four are pink, two are yellow, and the rest are blue. After playing outside all week, they're all so dirty you can't tell what color they are any more. Getting them cleaned cost Priddy's mom a total of $64 dollars. All the dresses cost the same amount to clean. What is the cost for cleaning just the blue ones

113. Burt Luvre has three parrots. Kritter and Gooberhead got into a bell-ringing contest. Kritter can ring his bell 15 times in 5 seconds. Gooberhead can ring his 100 times in one minute. Meanwhile, Squawker just looked at them both like they were crazy. Who rings their bell the most in one hour?

114. If a woodchuck could chuck wood, I suspect a woodchuck would chuck 5 pieces of wood every ten minutes. If I employ a woodchuck to chuck wood for forty hours, how much wood would a woodchuck chuck if a woodchuck could chuck wood?

115. There are fifteen elephants in a parade. Each elephant is carrying two riders. Each rider has two dogs in his arms. How many legs are there in the parade?

Basic Math

116. Grey Bird collects feathers to make into hats. He needs five hundred feathers for one hat. He has one hat already and orders for a total of five hats. How many more feathers does he need?

117. Huey Yupp made 2 bags for his mom to carry groceries in. The material cost $1 per yard. Huey needed 3 1/2 feet to make the bags. How much material did Huey have to buy? How much did it cost? When Huey went to the store later that week, he found the same kind of bag on sale for $5 each. Did he save money by making the bags himself?

118. There are fifteen bags of fruit on the shelf. Each bag contains four apples, five oranges, three grapefruits, and ninety-six grapes. There are twenty kids in the class. If the teacher divided all the fruit evenly among the students, how many pieces does each person get?

119. Sam Yule is in a race with his sister to see who can finish their math homework first. She has 25 problems to do. He has 38 of his own problems to do. In the time it takes for her to answer 2 problems, he can answer 3. Who will win?

Basic Math

120. Bonnie Rabutt and Ken Null decide to go into business together. Bonnie is going to open a new rabbit-sitter service, and Ken will provide the happy bunnies with entertainment by doing Charlie Chaplin impersonations. Food is going to cost them $50 per month. They each want to make $25 per month. If Bonnie's rabbit cages can hold 10 rabbits, what is the least amount of money they should charge for rabbit-sitting every month?

Decimals

121. There's a new restaurant in town called Three Dog Nite. People can go out to eat and take their dogs with them. Dog food costs the restaurant $.84 per plate. How much are they charging if they make $5.12 in profits for each plate of dog food?

122. Allie Jence bought seven and eight tenths meters of material for a dress. When Allie got home, she changed her mind and decided to make a shirt and a skirt. The shirt takes three and fifty-two hundredths of a meter of material. The skirt takes four and two hundredths of a meter of material. Does she have enough material?

Basic Math

123. Abby Normal is buying everything she can find in a craft store that costs less than a dollar. She bought six things that cost fifty cents each, five things that cost forty cents each, and thirteen things that cost two for fifty cents. How much money did she spend?

124. Chu Yerfood and five friends met for dinner last night. Each of them paid fifteen dollars and ten cents for dinner. How much money did they spend altogether?

125. Mac N. Cheese is making a lunch run to a McD's this afternoon. After he takes everyone's order, Ms. Understand gives him $10. Ms. Demeanor gives him $5. Ms. Begotten gives him $15. Ms. Turry gives him $3. Mac didn't order anything at McD's. The total cost was $27.46. How much money did the clerk give back to Mac?

126. Bill Offgoods has a collection of comic books. Every week, he gets an allowance of $15 because he does a lot of chores around the house and keeps his grades up. Comic books cost $2.95 each. How many comic books can he get each month (4 weeks)?

Basic Math

127. Gerry Rigged has a huge pen. The pen holds 43 mL of ink. If Gerry uses .33 mL of ink every day, how many full days will his pen last?

128. Lucky Kidd has nineteen dollars and ninety-eight cents. He paid five dollars and eight cents for a ceramic bird. Then he paid twelve dollars and seventy-two cents for a used CD by Kansas. Next, he found his friend, who paid him back the seven dollars and fifty-three cents she owed him. So, he went to lunch and paid six dollars and forty-seven cents for salad. How much money does Lucky have left?

129. Dolly Haus got some money for her birthday. As a joke, everyone gave her coins. Her aunt gave her five nickels and twenty dimes. Her sister gave her five dimes and twenty nickels. Her brother gave her five hundred pennies. Then Dolly went out to buy a toy that cost four dollars and ninety-eight cents and some gum for seventy-five cents. How much money does she have left?

130. Jack Squat can use either hairspray or gel to make his hair spike in front. Hairspray costs $0.09 per ounce, and each time he does his hair, he uses .75 ounces if he uses hairspray. Gel costs $0.05 per ounce, and each time he does his hair, he uses 2.2 ounces if he uses gel. Which would cost him the least to use per day?

Basic Math

131. Gummy Wurms went to a candy store to get a snack. He picked up a pack of jellybeans for $3.12 and a pack of sour apples for $2.98. He has 52 quarters in his wallet. Does he have enough to pay for the candy?

132. Dov Coat is saving up his money to buy a new jacket with the name of his favorite football team on it. The jacket will cost him $193.73. He mowed 7 yards over the summer for $20 each. How much money does he still need to get?

133. Stu Meet is cooking dinner for eighteen of his closest friends. Each person's dinner cost $5.31 for the meat, $8.32 dollars for the vegetables, and $2.39 for dessert. How much did Stu spend for dinner for himself and his friends?

134. Amaya Hayr got some new hair jewelry. She picked up 2 sets of hair picks for $1.99 each, and five beaded hair scrunchies for $3.20 each. What was the total cost for her new hair jewelry?

Basic Math

135. Drew Pixer is collecting doodles other people have made. He currently has a collection of 48 doodles. Skippy D'Lou offers to pay him $.12 for each of his doodles. How much money would he have if he sold half his doodles?

136. Daisy wants to open a flower shop. She's deciding on the name of the shop. She wants to call it Daisy's Daisies or Oopsie-Daisies. It all comes down to the price of the sign. The sign maker charges $4.83 for each letter that has curves and $9.32 for each letter that has no curves. Punctuation, like apostrophes and hyphens will cost $2.48 each. Which sign will cost less?

137. Moe Tersicle bought an electronic toy for his cat. This toy is a self-propelled motorcycle just like his and has a dangling fuzzball on the back for the cat to chase. The toy cost $28.83. If his allowance is $1.50 a week, how long did it take for him to save the money?

138. Burt Sede has $25. He went to the store and bought a toothbrush for $2.13, 12 bananas for $.30 each, a bag of bird seed for $5.32, and a toy for his parrot for $4.86. When he handed the clerk his money, how much did he get back?

Basic Math

139. Every month, Ben Kerr manages to save $100.38. In December, he manages to save an additional $2.84. How much money does he save in a year?

140. Sam U. Well and Ari Ull had big dreams of opening their own lemonade stands for the summer. Over the course of the summer, Sam sold 4,829 cups of lemonade for 5 cents per cup. Ari sold 52 gallons of lemonade for $1 per gallon. Who made the most money?

141. Jose Kanyusee won some money in a shoe-tying contest. To celebrate, he took his mom, dad, and brother out to dinner and a movie. After all was said and done, he had exactly enough money left to buy a CD for $15.93. The movie cost $9 per person. Dinner cost $12.95 per person. How much money did he win in the contest?

142. Zane Neekid has a weird hobby. He does critter impersonations on stage. Every Saturday, he performs for all his friends. Tickets to his performances cost $0.05. If he averages 10 members of the audience every Saturday, about how much money does he make in one year to the nearest dollar?

Basic Math

143. Billy Gote has sixty-nine matchbox cars. For his birthday, his four friends chip in and buy him more matchbox cars. The cars cost one dollar and forty-nine cents each. If each friend contributed five dollars and forty cents, how many matchbox cars does Billy have after his birthday?

144. Paige Turner's dad loves the University of Texas. She is playing a trick on her dad for his birthday. She got him a Texas A&M T-shirt, an A&M coffee cup, and an A&M pencil. The shirt cost $21.20. The coffee cup cost $4.27. She got back $2.19 from 3 $10 bills. How much did the pencil cost?

Estimations, Range

145. The wild birds at Willy Feedem's house go through a bunch of seeds, but they always leave the hulls behind. One day, they ate 383 seeds. The second day, they ate 689 seeds. The third day, they ate 384 seeds. To the nearest hundred, how many total seeds did they eat in the three days?

146. Mai Callangelo became bored over the summer and decided to paint the blades of grass in her yard orange. While painting, she counted 20,000 blades of grass in her front yard. The backyard is twice as large. What is a reasonable estimate for the number of blades of grass in the back yard?

Basic Math

147. Fred got bored one afternoon and counted dust particles in his house. His kitchen had four million, seventeen thousand, thirty-two dust particles. His living room had five hundred fifty-six million, nine hundred two thousand, five hundred fifty dust particles. His bedroom had seven hundred thirty-eight million, four thousand, three hundred two dust particles. To the nearest million, approximately how many dust particles are there in Fred's house?

148. Dawg Gonnit has lost his dog. He decides to make full-color posters to put up around town. Each poster costs $1.95 to make. If he has $20, about how many posters can he make?

149. Ella Gants is going to move soon. She has to pack all of her books into four boxes. Whatever doesn't fit in the four boxes has to be donated to a charity. Each box can contain twenty-seven books. What is the best estimate of the number of books Ella can pack?

150. Mary Krismiss is going to buy a bunch of toys for her Pomeranian for Christmas. She has $20 to use to buy dog toys. The toys cost $2.50 each. Using rounding or compatible numbers, what's the best estimate of the number of toys Mary can get?

Basic Math

151. Ida Hoe's dog likes to eat dry dog food, but she's weird. She eats clusters of the little pellets. One day, she ate 3,392 pellets. The next day she ate 358 pellets. The third day, she ate 2,759 pellets. The fourth day, she ate 8,529 pellets. The fifth day, she ate 2,859 pellets. To the nearest thousand, how many total pellets did she eat in the five days?

152. Every day, Johnny B. Good's bird, Munchkin, eats his pellets. He eats exactly 3,728 pellets per day. Round that to the nearest thousand and find out approximately how much Munchkin eats by the end of the week.

153. Jerry Mander has 2 dogs. Dot eats 143 pellets every day. Spot, though, is so busy being silly, he only eats 78 pellets every day. After figuring out how many total pellets they eat in one day, round that to the nearest hundred. Then figure out how many total pellets they eat in 3 days and round to the nearest thousand.

154. Gene has four tomato plants. The puniest plant has four tomatoes on it. The most impressive plant has sixteen on it. Within what range will the total number of tomatoes fall?

Basic Math

155. Betty Khan has a bunch of safety pins with beads on them. Each bead means something. She has four hundred fifty-two blue beads that mean "friendship." She has fifty-two red beads that mean "I don't like you." She has sixty-nine thousand pink beads that mean "love." She has fourteen green beads that mean "Go away already." To the nearest thousand, how many beads does she have?

156. Daisy is going to give her mom a big bunch of flowers. She bought 4 carnations for $.78 each and 10 roses for $2.23 each. Round the money to the nearest dollar then find the best estimate of the amount of money Daisy spent.

157. Avi Dreeder has 200 books in his collection. If each book cost him $6.99, about how much did he spend for all his books?

158. Eighteen pairs of bears of bears had 19 cubs in one year. If this continued every year for 5 years and none of the bears died, how many total bears would there be at the end of 5 years? After you find that answer, round to the nearest 10.

Basic Math

159. June Ipper's dog jumps about three hundred times per hour. He jumps about 15-18 inches each time. If she adds all the distances he jumps, without rounding or using compatible numbers between jumps, what is the maximum and minimum number of feet he jumps in one hour?

160. Molly Cottle is buying fish for her fish tank. Each fish is seventy-five cents. She has ten dollars. If you round the money to the nearest dollar, approximately how many fish will she end up getting?

161. Annie Malluver ran for the office of Chief Hamster Petter. If she wins, she gets to pet a hamster every day for 39 minutes. After rounding to the nearest half-hour, estimate how long would it take her to amass 15 hours of hamster petting time?

Basic Math

Fractions

162. Aaron Mitires and Cara Mehome got into a disagreement about which was larger ½ of a pizza or 5/10 of a pizza. Which one is bigger?

163. Gravity on Earth = 1. Gravity on the moon = 1/6 of Earth. Wayan Tonn weighs 100 pounds on Earth. He calculated his weight on the moon as about 17 pounds. How did he do that calculation?

Basic Math

164. Daisy made five batches of cookies when Miranda came over to play. Miranda and Daisy each ate five cookies. If there are 2 dozen cookies in a batch, write a mixed fraction and an improper fraction to represent how many dozens of cookies are left.

165. Rebecca broke a stick into sixty-two pieces. Each piece is ¾ inch long. How long was the original stick?

166. Kay Ick made a cake for the end of the year party. There were 60 pieces of the cake. The boys in the class ate 6/10 of the cake. The girls ate 2/5 of the cake. How many total pieces did the boys eat? How many total pieces did the girls eat? How many pieces are left?

167. Dot Yereyes is editing her friend's paper. For every four words of writing, she found a mistake. She found seventeen mistakes. Her friend found one mistake in Dot's paper for every ten words of writing. Dot's paper had ten mistakes. Who wrote the longest paper?

Basic Math

168. Doc Sooned is teaching his dachshund Spike how to play fetch. Spike will return the ball 5 times out of 7. How many times must Doc throw the ball to get the ball back 50 times?

169. Berry Pie's bird eats 2/5 of her mass every day in food. She eats 25 grams of food. What is her mass?

170. Bob Ingduck, Al Umminim, and Tyya Knot are in a race to see who can put a list of words in alphabetical order the fastest. Bob can organize 5 words every fifteen seconds. Al can organize 10 words every forty seconds. Tyya can organize 250 words in 5 minutes. Who wins?

Answer Key

Each problem is listed with the following information:
Difficulty: This is my best estimate of how difficult the problems are. The difficulty ranges from Very Easy (little, if any, brain power needed) to Very Hard (will require a lot of processing or combining information). Some problems were ranked with a higher complexity than may seem appropriate if the reading level in the problem looked a little high.
Skills Needed: This is a list of the skills the student must master to do the problem independently. If the student is weak in one or more skills, some scaffolding or extra help will be needed.
Problem: This is the actual challenge that you'll need to give the student.
Steps: I've given one solution strategy. In rare cases, I gave two strategies. If there was a calculation, I tried to write it out in mathematical terms, but the formatting limitations made this a bit challenging. If the equation started looking like a PhD in mathematics would be necessary, I also included a narrative version of what needed to happen. For some problems, there really isn't much in the way of steps to take.
Answer: The actual solution to the problem is here.
Tips for Modifying: I tried to give suggestions of ways to simplify or complicate the problem.

Basic Math

Number Sense

In the Number Sense section, there are questions and answers rather than word problems. These are ranked by how much the student must understand about the concept being covered to answer the question. You can modify these by changing the numbers to something simpler or trickier.

1.
Difficulty: Easy
Skills Needed: translating words to numbers, ordering, place value recognition.
Problem: On vacation, Bob traveled six hundred sixty-eight miles. Fred traveled five hundred fifteen miles. Skippy traveled four hundred ninety-one miles. George traveled six hundred eighty-four miles. Arrange the names from least to greatest distance traveled.
Steps: Translate the words to numbers. Put the numbers in order, smallest first.
Answer: Skippy, Fred, Bob, George
Tips for Modifying: For an easier problem, use smaller numbers or write all numbers in standard number form. For a harder problem, use numbers that go to higher place values or give some or all of the travelers side trips that add to their total mileage.

2.
Difficulty: Easy
Skills Needed: translating words to numbers, ordering, understanding place value
Problem: Lenny Monade owned a lemonade stand. On Saturday, he had one hundred eighty-four customers. On Friday, he had one hundred twenty-eight customers. On Monday, he had ninety-eight customers. On Wednesday, he had one hundred twelve customers. Order the days from the busiest to the slowest.
Steps: Translate the words to numbers. Put the numbers in order from greatest to least.
Answer: Saturday, Friday, Wednesday, Monday

Cindy Koepp

Tips for Modifying: For an easier problem, include fewer days or smaller numbers. For a harder problem, include more days or larger numbers.

3.
Q. What is the largest 4-digit number you can make without repeating digits or using consecutive digits anywhere in the number (adjacent or not)?
A. 9876

4.
Q. What is the smallest 4-digit number you can make without repeating digits or using consecutive digits anywhere in the number (adjacent or not)? No, you can't start with 0.
A. 1023

5.
Q. What is the largest 4-digit number you can make?
A. 9999

6.
Q. What is the smallest 4-digit number you can make? No, you can't start with 0.
A. 1000

7.
Q. What's wrong with this number? Fix the problem. Seventeen thousand, twelve hundred four
A. Twelve hundred isn't possible when there's already something in the thousands place. The fix for that is to write out all the parts: 17,000 and 1204. Then add them up (18,204). That'd be written Eighteen thousand, two hundred four.

8.
Q. Write four different 9-digit numbers that all have a 5 in the ten thousands place, a 7 in the hundreds place, and a 4 in the millions place. No repeating digits allowed

Basic Math

in the same number. Now put the numbers in order from greatest to least.
A. There are many valid answers, but here's one.
924,853,716
864,952,731
324,958,761
284,351,769

9.
Q. Which number is greater?
Seventy-two million, nine hundred four thousand, seven and two hundredths, or Seventy-two million, nine hundred forty thousand, seven and two hundredths
A. Seventy two million, nine hundred forty thousand, seven and two hundredths

10.
Q. Penny Sill has five pens and twelve pencils. Write the fact family for the number of writing implements Penny has.
A. 5+12=17, 12+5=17, 17-5=12, 17-12=5

11.
Q. What is the smallest 4-digit number you can make without repeating digits or using consecutive digits anywhere in the number (adjacent or not)? No, you can't start with 0.
A. 1357

12.
Q. What is the largest 4-digit number you can make without repeating digits or using consecutive digits anywhere in the number (adjacent or not)?
A. 9753

13.
Q. What numbers between 1 and 20 are prime?
A. 2, 3, 5, 7, 11, 13, 17, 19

14.
Q. What numbers between 1 and 25 have two or three for a factor?
A. 2, 3, 4, 6, 8, 9, 10, 12, 14, 15, 16, 18, 20, 21, 22, 24

15.
Q. Find all the factors of 256.
A. 1, 2, 4, 8, 16, 32, 64, 128, 256

16.
Q. If the prefix "mill-" means 1000, why are "millions" located where they are in a number?
A. Million is 1000 sets of 1000.

17.
Q. Why can't I have a place value occupied by a double-digit number (like 13 or 27)?
A. In place values, only one digit is allowed. The digit on the left belongs in the next place value up. Clarification: Twelve hundred becomes one thousand two hundred.

Basic Math

Basic Four-Functions

18.
Difficulty: Easy
Skills Needed: addition, translating words to numbers
Problem: Willy Quit likes to play his guitar for hours at a time. He played his guitar for five hours on Monday, six hours on Tuesday, Eight hours on Wednesday, two hours on Thursday, and ten hours on Friday. How many hours did he play his guitar that week?
Steps: 5 + 6 + 8 + 2 + 10 hrs
Answer: 31 hours
Tips for Modifying: For an easier problem, provide the numbers as digits or use numbers that are more compatible. For a harder problem, use more difficult numbers or include fractions of hours. Some times could be given in minutes or seconds.

19.
Difficulty: Easy
Skills Needed: multiplication, days/week, translating words to numbers
Problem: R.U. Done-Yet ran fifteen miles every day for one week. How many miles did he run?
Steps: 15 miles/day x 7 days
Answer: 105 miles
Tips for Modifying: For an easier problem, use a smaller number that involves a basic multiplication fact. For a harder problem, use larger numbers or give the distance in one unit and require the answer in another.

20.
Difficulty: Easy
Skills Needed: subtraction, translating words to numbers
Problem: Won Togo is stuffing his face with candy. He started with fifty-two pieces of candy and ate thirteen of them before Mom caught him. How many pieces are left?
Steps: 52 − 13

Answer: 39
Tips for Modifying: For an easier problem, use numbers that are more compatible. For a harder problem, use larger numbers or give the number of candies he can eat in one minute then give the number of minutes he spent eating before he was caught.

21.
Difficulty: Easy
Skills Needed: multiplication, translating numbers from words
Problem: Miya Frend picked up a new species of snake. This weirdo has all his scales in stripes. Each stripe has sixty scales. If there are thirty-two stripes, how many total scales are there?
Steps: 32 stripes x 60 scales/stripe
Answer: 1920 scales
Tips for Modifying: For an easier problem, use smaller or more-compatible numbers. For a harder problem, use larger numbers or break the total number of stripes into smaller groups, each having a different number of scales.

22.
Difficulty: Easy
Skills Needed: multiplication, translating words to numbers
Problem: Cookie Teal has a strange new kind of bird. This bird has five colors of feathers. Each color has ninety-two feathers. How many feathers are there altogether?
Steps: 5 colors x 92 feathers/color
Answer: 460 feathers
Tips for Modifying: For an easier problem, use smaller or more-compatible numbers. For a harder problem, give different numbers of feathers for each color or use larger numbers.

Basic Math

23.
Difficulty: Easy
Skills Needed: division, translating words to numbers
Problem: Zane Neepal picked up a new species of snake. This weirdo has all his scales in stripes. Each stripe has six scales. If there are ninety scales, how many total stripes are there?
Steps: 90 scales / 6 scales/stripe
Answer: 15 stripes
Tips for Modifying: For an easier problem, use smaller or more-compatible numbers. For a harder problem, use larger numbers.

24.
Difficulty: Easy
Skills Needed: division, translating words to numbers
Problem: Bert Tee has a strange new kind of bird. This bird has five colors of feathers. Each color has the same number of feathers. If there are one hundred twenty-five feathers altogether, how many of each color are there?
Steps: 125 feathers / 5 colors
Answer: 25 feathers/color
Tips for Modifying: For an easier problem, use numbers that are part of a basic multiplication fact. For a harder problem, use larger or less-compatible numbers.

25.
Difficulty: Easy
Skills Needed: multiplication, addition, translating words to numbers
Problem: Jo Ger ran twelve miles. The next day, Jo ran twice as far. How many miles did Jo run in two days?
Steps: 12 miles x 3 or (12 miles x 2) + 12
Answer: 36 miles
Tips for Modifying: For an easier problem, give the numbers as digits or use smaller numbers. For a harder problem, use larger numbers or decimals. You can also give the distance for one lap and the number of laps each day.

26.
Difficulty: Easy
Skills Needed: multiplication, addition
Problem: Mina Byrd's parrot ate fifty-eight pellets. The next day, he ate three times as much. How many pellets did he eat in two days?
Steps: 58 pellets x 4 or (58 x 3) + 58
Answer: 232 pellets
Tips for Modifying: For an easier problem, use smaller or more-compatible numbers. For a harder problem, divide the total pellets into groups by some characteristic like color, flavor, or shape. Give the number of pellets for each type.

27.
Difficulty: Easy
Skills Needed: division, translating words to numbers, recognizing useless information
Problem: Misty Rios is trying out for a part in the school play. If she gets the part she's hoping for, she'll have to memorize seventy-two lines. One of the other parts in the play has one hundred forty-four lines. The play is in eight weeks. How many lines must she memorize each week to be ready on time?
Steps: Discard 144 lines for the other part in the play since the question is only about Misty's part. So, that leaves: 72 lines / 8 wks
Answer: 9 lines/wk
Tips for Modifying: For an easier problem, give the numbers in standard number form or remove the useless information. For a harder problem, use numbers that aren't part of the basic multiplication facts or give Misty a day or two off during the rehearsal time.

28.
Difficulty: Easy
Skills Needed: addition, translating words to numbers and numbers to words
Problem: A certain forest covered fifty-eight thousand, four hundred seventy-five acres. Trees For You came out

Basic Math

and added another seventeen thousand fourteen acres of seedlings around the outside. When the trees grow up, how many acres will the forest cover? Write the answer in numbers and in words.
Steps: 58,475 + 17,014 Translate to words.
Answer: 75,489 or seventy-five thousand, four hundred eighty-nine
Tips for Modifying: For an easier problem, make the numbers smaller or more compatible, or write them in numbers. For a harder problem, use larger numbers with more place values and insert zeroes in the numbers. You can also subdivide the total number of trees into groups by tree type and then, in the question, don't list one of the tree types to be included in the total.

29.
Difficulty: Easy
Skills Needed: multiplication, comparing numbers, translating words to numbers
Problem: T-shirts cost nine dollars each. Lena Onme wants to buy ten T-shirts. If Lena has one hundred dollars in her pocket, can Lena buy the T-shirts?
Steps: $9/shirt x 10 shirts Compare to $100.
Answer: Yes.
Tips for Modifying: For an easier problem, give the numbers in standard number form or ask for the total rather than comparing to a set amount. For a harder problem, use numbers that are not basic multiplication facts or include cents in the cost per shirt. You can also list different types or colors of shirt and give each a different cost and number purchased.

30.
Difficulty: Easy
Skills Needed: division, addition, translating words to numbers
Problem: Rocky Cliff dug up seven hundred thousand pebbles. Billy Gote dug up thirty-five thousand, two hundred six pebbles. They each put half their pebbles in a bucket. How many pebbles are in the bucket?

Steps: (700,000 / 2) + (35,206 / 2) or (700,000 + 35,206) / 2
Answer: 367,603 pebbles
Tips for Modifying: For an easier problem, use smaller numbers or write all numbers in standard number form. For a harder problem, use larger numbers and fractions other than half.

31.
Difficulty: Easy
Skills Needed: division, addition, translating words into numbers
Problem: Joe Kerr had seven hundred sixteen matchbox cars. For his birthday, his aunt gave him one half as many. How much does Joe have now?
Steps: (716 / 2) + 716 or 716 x 1.5
Answer: 1074 cars
Tips for Modifying: For an easier problem, use smaller, more-compatible numbers or write all numbers in standard number form. For a harder problem, split the total number of cars into types like color or body style or size. Give a number for each type. You can also use a fraction other than half or use larger, less-compatible numbers.

32.
Difficulty: Easy
Skills Needed: addition, subtraction, translating words to numbers and numbers to words
Problem: Mary Bell had four thousand, eighty-two marbles. She purchased two hundred seventy more at one store and sold one thousand six hundred five at a garage sale. Write how many she has now in words.
Steps: 4082 + 270 - 1605, Translate into words
Answer: 2747 or two thousand, seven hundred forty-seven
Tips for Modifying: For an easier problem, use smaller, more-compatible numbers. For a harder problem, use bigger numbers or divide the marbles into groups by color or type and give the amounts she starts

Basic Math

with, buys, and sells for each type. Ask for the total marbles in the end.

33.
Difficulty: Easy
Skills Needed: multiplication, addition, translating words to numbers
Problem: Maya Cann saved sixty-eight cans for recycling. Uri Cann saved four times as many as Emily did. How many cans do they have altogether?
Steps: 68 x 5 or (68 x 4) + 68
Answer: 340 cans
Tips for Modifying: For an easier problem, use smaller, more-compatible numbers. For a harder problem, give the amount he saved as a fraction or mixed number of hers.

34.
Difficulty: Easy
Skills Needed: division (or multiplying by a fraction)
Problem: The gravity on the moon is 1/6 of that on Earth. Astro Knott weighs 105 pounds on Earth. What would Astro weigh on the moon?
Steps: 105 / 6 x 1
Answer: 17 1/2 pounds
Tips for Modifying: For an easier problem, use a number more compatible with 1/6. For a harder problem, make up an alien world that has a more interesting fraction for gravity, such as 3/5 or 7/4.

35.
Difficulty: Easy
Skills Needed: division
Problem: Wheelan Axel really likes to write. One story he wrote was 120,000 words long. No kidding. If he can write 200 words on a page, how many pages long was it?
Steps: 120,000 / 200
Answer: 600 pages
Tips for Modifying: For an easier problem, use smaller numbers. For a harder problem, use numbers

that are less compatible. You can also do things like mention the number of chapters and the number of words on the first and last page of a chapter.

36.
Difficulty: Easy
Skills Needed: multiplication
Problem: Hattie Molly eats jalapeños faster than anyone. If she can eat a jalapeno in 35 seconds, how long did it take her to eat 25 jalapenos?
Steps: 35 sec/jalapeno x 25 jalapenos
Answer: 875 seconds
Tips for Modifying: For an easier problem, use smaller numbers. For a harder problem, require the answer in a different unit.

37.
Difficulty: Easy
Skills Needed: multiplication, converting time units
Problem: Sally Kritter has a crazy little bird. She makes spitballs at the rate of 5 per minute. If she did that for 1 hour, how many spitballs would she make?
Steps: 5 spitballs/min x 60 min/hr
Answer: 300 spitballs/hour
Tips for Modifying: For an easier problem, change the hours to minutes. For a harder problem, use larger, less-compatible numbers.

38.
Difficulty: Easy
Skills Needed: addition, even/odd
Problem: What is the sum of the first 20 even numbers (starting with 0)?
Steps: 0 + 2 + 4 + 6 + 8 + 10 + 12 + 14 + 16 + 18 + 20 + 22 + 24 + 26 + 28 + 30 + 32 + 34 + 36 + 38
Answer: 380
Tips for Modifying: For an easier problem, use a smaller number of even numbers or provide a chart showing the even and odd numbers. For a harder problem, change the operation, require more numbers,

or pick a different starting point. You could even start with a negative number.

39.
Difficulty: Easy
Skills Needed: division
Problem: Mike Arr loves to write stories. Every night after finishing his homework, Mike works on his latest novel, Running Tally, which is about a girl nicknamed Tally who solves crimes by chasing down the bad guys. The average novel is 90,000 words. If Mike finishes his novel in 300 days, how many words did he write each day?
Steps: 90,000 words / 300 days
Answer: 300 words per day
Tips for Modifying: For an easier problem, use smaller numbers or take out the extraneous story information about the plot of his book. For a harder problem, make the numbers less compatible.

40.
Difficulty: Easy
Skills Needed: addition, multiplication, translating words to numbers
Problem: Dot Maytricks is having problems with her printer. Every time she sends a file to be printed, the printer shoots out an extra page with random spots on it. She discovered this problem at the end of the day. If she had printed sixteen files that day and each file was a page long, how many pages came out of the printer?
Steps: (1 page file + 1 extra page of dots) x 16 printouts
Answer: 32 pages
Tips for Modifying: For an easier problem, put the numbers standard number form or remove unnecessary story elements. For a harder problem, make the numbers larger or vary the size of some of the files printed.

41.
Difficulty: Easy
Skills Needed: days in a month, division, dealing with remainders, translating words to numbers
Problem: Al LeGator has a type of lizard called a caiman. Al's lizard eats one chicken drumstick every day. Drumsticks come in packages of ten. How many packages does Al have to buy to keep his caiman fed for the month of October?
Steps: 31 days in October / 10 drumsticks in a package. Round all remainders up because you can't buy a fractional package of chicken.
Answer: 4 packages of chicken
Tips for Modifying: For an easier problem, choose a month that has a number of days divisible by 10 or give all numbers in standard number form. For a harder problem, change the number of drumsticks per package.

42.
Difficulty: Easy
Skills Needed: subtraction, translating words to numbers, comparing numbers
Problem: In 2014, Ella Jibble wants to be a member of a band, but she has to be at least fourteen years old. She was born two years after her brother, who was born in 1999. Is Ella old enough in 2014?
Steps: 2014 - (1999 + 2) Compare the answer to 14.
Answer: No. In 2014, she's only 13 years old.
Tips for Modifying: For an easier problem, rearrange the date and age requirement so the numbers are more compatible. Give all numbers in standard number form. For a harder problem, rearrange the date and age requirements to end up with less-compatible numbers.

43.
Difficulty: Easy
Skills Needed: multiplication, translating words to numbers, comparing numbers
Problem: Steve needs to collect forty-five cans for a recycling project. Each person on his block gives him

four cans. If there are fifteen people on his block, did he reach his goal?
Steps: 15 people x 4 cans/person. Compare to 45.
Answer: Yes.
Tips for Modifying: For an easier problem, give all numbers in standard number form or use more-compatible numbers. For a harder problem, use larger, less-compatible numbers or create subgroups of his neighbors (blue houses, have kids, own a dog, etc) and vary the number of cans he gets from the subgroups.

44.
Difficulty: Easy
Skills Needed: multiplication, subtraction, days in a week
Problem: Kit T. Littur hates cleaning up after her cat, Lunchmeat. Kit wants to hire her little brother to do it. If Kit makes $10 babysitting every night and needs $20 a week for herself, what is the maximum she could offer her brother to clean up after Lunchmeat every week?
Steps: ($10/night x 7 nights/wk) - $20
Answer: $50
Tips for Modifying: For an easier problem, use smaller numbers. For a harder problem, make the numbers less compatible or add some cents to the amounts. You could also add other income sources or other expenses.

45.
Difficulty: Easy
Skills Needed: multiplication, translating words to numbers
Problem: Kat Agorey is a player in a game show. She has to pick from one of five categories of questions. Each category has six questions. Each question has four possible answer choices. How many total answer choices are there?
Steps: 5 categories x 6 questions/category x 4 answer choices/question
Answer: 120 answer choices

Tips for Modifying: For an easier problem, give all numbers in standard number form or use smaller numbers. For a harder problem, use bigger numbers or add in information about how many questions have already been eliminated.

46.
Difficulty: Easy
Skills Needed: division, using decimals
Problem: Alexus is running a lemonade stand. Her goal is to make $10. She made enough lemonade for 25 cups. If she sells it all, what will she have to charge to make her goal?
Steps: $10 total / 25 cups
Answer: 40 cents
Tips for Modifying: For an easier problem, use smaller or more-compatible numbers. For a harder problem, use larger or less-compatible numbers. You can also add in additional information like cookies for sale.

47.
Difficulty: Easy
Skills Needed: multiplication
Problem: Connie Book has 100 comic books. Each comic book has 72 pages. How many total pages are in the comic books?
Steps: 100 comic books x 72 pages/comic book
Answer: 7200 pages
Tips for Modifying: For an easier problem, use smaller numbers. For a harder problem, use larger numbers or divide the comics into groups that each have a different number of pages. For example, say that X-Men comics have 64 pages, Spider-Man comics have 72 pages, and Superman comics have 56 pages. Then give the number of each kind of comic book he has.

48.
Difficulty: Easy
Skills Needed: division, dealing with useless information

Basic Math

Problem: Ted E. Behr has 750 tiny teddy bears. Each one is less than 2" tall. His dad made him a special cabinet to keep them all in. Since he started his tiny teddy bear collection, Ted has received 2 bears every week. For how many weeks has he been collecting tiny teddy bears?
Steps: 750 tiny teddy bears / 2 tiny teddy bears/wk
Answer: 375 weeks
Tips for Modifying: For an easier problem, use smaller numbers or get rid of the extraneous information. For a harder problem, use less-compatible numbers or introduce other information such as the number of tiny teddy bears he got for his birthday in addition to the usual number per week.

49.
Difficulty: Easy
Skills Needed: multiplication
Problem: Reid Bukes reads one chapter in a book every day. Each chapter has about 1000 words in it. If the book has 14 chapters, how many words are there?
Steps: 1000 words/chapter x 14 chapters
Answer: 14,000 words
Tips for Modifying: For an easier problem, use smaller numbers. For a harder problem, use less-compatible numbers or increase the number of books, some of which may have more or fewer words per chapter.

50.
Difficulty: Easy
Skills Needed: multiplication
Problem: Grey Nola eats 5 granola bars for a snack at school every day. He's in school every day for 200 days. How many total granola bars does he eat?
Steps: 5 granolas/day x 200 days/school year
Answer: 1000 granola bars per school year
Tips for Modifying: For an easier problem, use smaller numbers. For a harder problem, use numbers that are less compatible or introduce other information

such as varying the number he eats on different days of the week or other types of snacks he eats on some occasions.

51.
Difficulty: Easy
Skills Needed: addition, division, dealing with remainders
Problem: Miss Understand wants to divide her students into groups of 4 each for a project. There are 8 boys and 14 girls in the class. How many groups will there be? If there are unassigned students, what does she do with them?
Steps: (8 boys + 14 girls) / 4 kids/group
Answer: There will be 5 groups of 4 and one group of 2 or 3 groups of 4 and two groups of 5.
Tips for Modifying: For an easier problem, use more-compatible numbers to get rid of the remainder. For a harder problem, use larger numbers or assign other criteria, such as each group must contain a certain number of boys or girls.

52.
Difficulty: Easy
Skills Needed: division with decimals in the answer
Problem: Miles Togo is going skiing. He buys five bottles of water for the day. He spent a total of $22 for the water. How much did each bottle of water cost?
Steps: $22 / 5 bottles
Answer: $4.40 per water bottle
Tips for Modifying: For an easier problem, use numbers that won't leave decimals in the answer. For a harder problem, include cents in the total cost or add information about snacks he also purchased.

53.
Difficulty: Easy
Skills Needed: division, translating words to numbers, dealing with remainders

Basic Math

Problem: Alexus has two hundred six pieces of cake. She planned to have just enough for each guest at the party to have four pieces of cake. How many guests is she expecting?
Steps: 206 pieces / 4 pieces/person
Answer: 51 guests with 2 extra pieces of cake
Tips for Modifying: For an easier problem, use numbers that won't leave a remainder or use smaller numbers or give all numbers in standard number form. For a harder problem, make the numbers larger or introduce extraneous information like the amount of ice cream or soda.

54.
Difficulty: Easy
Skills Needed: division, dealing with remainders, translating words to numbers
Problem: Tyya has sixty-two bird feathers. She needs four for an art project. How many of those projects can she do? If she has leftovers, what should she do with them?
Steps: 62 / 4
Answer: 15 projects with 2 extra feathers. For the extras, any logical answer will do. Examples: Give them to a friend, keep them for next time, or throw them away.
Tips for Modifying: For an easier problem, give all numbers in standard number form or use compatible numbers. For a harder problem, use larger numbers or divide the feathers into categories (e.g.: red ones, skinny ones, extra fuzzy ones, etc.) that must be added to find the total number of feathers.

55.
Difficulty: Easy
Skills Needed: addition, multiplication, translating words to numbers
Problem: Penny Pensill has five boxes of green pens and two boxes of black pens. Each box, regardless of

color, contains twenty-four pens. How many total pens does she have?
Steps: (5 + 2) x 24
Answer: 168 pens
Tips for Modifying: For an easier problem, use more-compatible numbers or give all numbers in standard number form. For a harder problem, vary the number of pens in a box by color, add more colors of pens, or make the numbers larger.

56.
Difficulty: Easy
Skills Needed: division, translating words to numbers, dealing with remainders
Problem: Penny Ferthots has thirty-three fuzzy pencil cushions. She's tired of them and wants to get rid of them by splitting them evenly among her four friends. How many does each friend get? If there are extras, what does Penny do with them?
Steps: 33 pencil cushions / 4 friends Keep the remainder.
Answer: 8 cushions per friend
Tips for Modifying: For an easier problem, give all numbers in standard number form or use more-compatible numbers that won't leave remainders. For a harder problem, use larger numbers or instead of giving the total number of pencil cushions she started with, divide it up into categories (green, striped, fuzzy, squishy, etc.) that must be added together to get to the total.

57.
Difficulty: Easy
Skills Needed: division
Problem: Kameron has a collection of baseball caps. Each cap has a logo made with 2000 stitches. There are 2,634,000 stitches in his baseball cap collection. How many baseball caps does he have?
Steps: 2,634,000 stitches in all / 2000 stitches
Answer: 1317 caps

Basic Math

Tips for Modifying: For an easier problem, use smaller numbers. For a harder problem, use larger or less-compatible numbers with fewer zeroes.

58.
Difficulty: Easy
Skills Needed: expanded form, division
Problem: Herb Plant wrote the following expanded number on his paper: 30000+200+3. What is that number divided by 4?
Steps: Compile the expanded number back into the normal form. 30203 / 4
Answer: 7550 remainder 3 or 7550.75
Tips for Modifying: For an easier problem, make the expanded number smaller. For a harder problem, make the expanded number more involved.

59.
Difficulty: Easy
Skills Needed: multiplication, translating words to numbers, addition
Problem: Perry Yitt has twelve toys for big parrots in his house. Each one costs about twenty dollars. He also has five toys for small parrots in his house. Each one costs about fifteen dollars. How much did he spend for all his parrot toys?
Steps: (12 x $20) + (5 x $15)
Answer: $315
Tips for Modifying: For an easier problem, use smaller numbers or give all numbers in standard number form. For a harder problem, use less-compatible numbers or add cents to the dollar amounts.

60.
Difficulty: Easy
Skills Needed: division, dealing with remainders
Problem: There are one hundred seventeen kids and ten adults going on a field trip. One bus can hold fifty people, not counting the bus driver. How many buses will be needed?

Steps: (117 + 10) / 50 Round all remainders up because you can't have a fractional bus.
Answer: 3 buses
Tips for Modifying: For an easier problem, use more compatible or smaller numbers. For a harder problem, use larger or less-compatible numbers or include information about some people traveling in their own car, so they get taken out of the total.

61.
Difficulty: Easy
Skills Needed: multiplication, dealing with useless information, translating words to numbers
Problem: There are eighty-five elephants and twelve zebras in a parade. If each zebra has twenty-eight black stripes, how many ears are in the parade?
Steps: (85 + 12) x 2.
Answer: 194 ears
Tips for Modifying: For an easier problem, give all numbers in standard number form or remove the extraneous information. For a harder problem, include more critters, use larger numbers, include more useless information. You could also include things like people riding on the elephants and zebras carrying smaller critters.

62.
Difficulty: Easy
Skills Needed: division, dealing with remainders, translating words to numbers
Problem: Mr. E. Meet has 133 pencils. His class has twenty kids. How many pencils will each kid get if everyone gets the same amount?
Steps: 133 pencils / 20 kids Mr. E. keeps the remainder.
Answer: 6 pencils per kid
Tips for Modifying: For an easier problem, give numbers in standard number form or use compatible or smaller numbers. For a harder problem, use larger numbers. Instead of giving the total pencils up front,

Basic Math

break the total into groups (purple, sparkly, etc.) so the total pencils have to be calculated.

63.
Difficulty: Easy
Skills Needed: addition, division, translating words to numbers
Problem: Ima Nutt asked her mom and dad for pieces of ribbon for her friends. Each parent gave her twelve pieces of ribbon. If she has six friends and they all get the same number of pieces, how many ribbons will each friend get?
Steps: $(12 + 12) / 6$
Answer: 4 pieces
Tips for Modifying: For an easier problem, give all numbers in standard number form or give the total number of pieces she gets from her parents. For a harder problem, vary the number of ribbon pieces she gets from each of her parents. Toss in some extra relatives who give her ribbon and maybe include someone who gives her something else to introduce some extraneous information. Use larger, less-compatible numbers.

64.
Difficulty: Easy
Skills Needed: addition, dealing with useless information
Problem: Rex Cars loves kumquats. The first time he went to the store, he bought 18 kumquats. The second time, he bought 17. He bought none the third time but picked up a lovely bunch of 58 coconuts. How many kumquats did Rex get altogether?
Steps: $18 + 17$ Ignore the coconuts.
Answer: 35 kumquats
Tips for Modifying: For an easier problem, use smaller or more-compatible numbers. For a harder problem, use bigger numbers or give one day as an operation based on another. For example, on the second day, he got five times more than he did on the first day.

65.
Difficulty: Easy
Skills Needed: subtraction, addition, division
Problem: Ima Loon likes to play football. On Monday, she caught 106 passes. On Tuesday, she caught 48 fewer passes. On Wednesday she caught 93 passes, and on Thursday she caught a third as many as she did on Wednesday. What is the difference between the total number of passes caught on Monday and Wednesday and the total number of passes caught on Tuesday and Thursday?
Steps: (106 + 93) - ((106-48) + (93 / 3))
Answer: 110 passes
Tips for Modifying: For an easier problem, use smaller or more-compatible numbers or remove the Wednesday and Thursday information. For a harder problem, use larger numbers or give Wednesday's passes as a function of Monday or Tuesday.

66.
Difficulty: Easy
Skills Needed: division, dealing with remainders
Problem: Candy Kane has 247 candies that she wants to distribute equally to her nieces and nephews but only if they come to her house to help her with a project. She has a total of 6 nieces and nephews, but she has no idea how many will come help. Fill in a chart to show the number of candies her nieces and nephews will get if they come over.
Steps: 247 / 6 or 247 / 5 or 247 / 4 or 247 / 3 or 247 / 2 or 247 / 1 Drop all remainders. Make a chart of the results.
Answer: 6 show up = 41 candies each, 5 show up = 49 candies each, 4 show up = 61 candies each, 3 show up = 82 candies each, 2 show up = 123 candies each, 1 shows up = 247 candies
Tips for Modifying: For an easier problem, have a smaller number of nieces and nephews or a number more compatible with the divisors, like 300. For a

harder problem, use larger number. You can also set up a situation where the nieces and nephews earn X candies for Y hours of work then list out how long each one worked.

67.
Difficulty: Easy
Skills Needed: multiplication
Problem: You're helping a little kid with homework. He needs to multiply 84x37, but he doesn't know how. Explain one way to do it without looking up the answer in a table or chart.
Steps: Any step-by-step walk through of the problem using a valid strategy. For example, using partial products, (4x7) + (4 x 30) + (80 x 7) + (80 x 30)
Answer: 3108 is the final answer.
Tips for Modifying: For an easier problem, use single-digit factors or more-compatible numbers. For a harder problem, require 2 or more strategies or larger numbers.

68.
Difficulty: Easy
Skills Needed: division, translating numbers to words and words to numbers
Problem: Rhode Island is the smallest state in the United States. Twice the area is two thousand, four hundred eight square miles. Write the area of Rhode Island in words.
Steps: 2408 / 2 Translated to words
Answer: 1204 square miles or one thousand two hundred four square miles
Tips for Modifying: For an easier problem, give the numbers in standard number form or give the simple area for Rhode Island. For a harder problem, give the area of Rhode Island then attach a bunch of operations to it like double it, add 84x83, subtract 972 divided by 7, and then write that in words.

69.
Difficulty: Easy-Moderate
Skills Needed: division, converting minutes to hours
Problem: Brett Less ran 8 miles. It took him 2 hours. If he ran the same speed the whole way, how far did he run in 60 minutes?
Steps: (60 min/ 60 min/hr) x (8 miles / 2 hours)
Answer: 4 miles
Tips for Modifying: For an easier problem, give both times in the same unit. For a harder problem, require a change in units for the answer or have the student calculate the speed Brett ran.

70.
Difficulty: Easy-Moderate
Skills Needed: division, translating words to numbers
Problem: X. Sample has eight dogs. Her unfortunate dogs have fleas. If each dog had the same number of fleas, how many fleas were there on each dog if there were two hundred fifty-six total fleas?
Steps: 256 fleas total / 8 dogs
Answer: 32 fleas per dog
Tips for Modifying: For an easier problem, use smaller, more-compatible numbers or give all numbers in standard number form. For a harder problem, use larger numbers or throw in some odd characteristics. For example, mention the size of the dogs and vary the number of fleas for each size. So, if there are some small dogs and some large dogs then the large dogs have twice as many fleas as the small ones, or something of that sort.

71.
Difficulty: Easy-Moderate
Skills Needed: writing the date in number form, division
Problem: Write today's date. Remove the punctuation. Divide by 15.
Steps and Answer: Depends on the date. For example, if today were October 10, 2012, the number form of that

Basic Math

would be 10/10/2012. Removing punctuation gives you 10,102,012. Dividing by 15 would get 673,467 with a remainder of 7.
Tips for Modifying: For an easier problem, use an easier operation or a smaller number. For a harder problem, use a larger number or multiple operations such as divide by 15, add 12, and subtract the date of (some major event being studied in history).

72.
Difficulty: Easy-Moderate
Skills Needed: division, multiplication
Problem: Moe Zart sees 5 little stars twinkle-twinkling in the sky in what appears to be a 3 square-inch area. If Moe can see a 15 square-inch area, how many little stars does Moe see twinkle-twinkling in all?
Steps: (5 stars / 3 sq in) x 15 sq in
Answer: 25 stars
Tips for Modifying: For an easier problem, make the small area 1 square inch. For a harder problem, use large numbers.

73.
Difficulty: Easy-Moderate
Skills Needed: division, logical reasoning, comparing numbers, multiplication
Problem: Perry Itt has a bird named Fuzzball. Fuzzball is molting or shedding feathers. She's shedding 1 feather every two days. She grows in 7 feathers a week. Will she lose all her feathers?
Steps: 7 / 2 compare to 7
Answer: No. She only loses 3.5 feathers per week.
Tips for Modifying: For an easier problem, use more-compatible numbers so there aren't fractions. For a harder problem, use larger or less-compatible numbers.

74.
Difficulty: Easy-Moderate
Skills Needed: time conversions, multiplication, division

Problem: Chip R. Chirper has a bird named Mouthy. Mouthy practiced his vocabulary by running through his entire library of sound effects and words. He didn't repeat anything. If he practiced for an hour and a half and managed one word or sound effect every two seconds, how many words and sound effects does he know?

Steps: ((((1 hour x 60 min/hr x 60 sec/min) / 2) + (1 hour x 60 min/hr x 60 sec/min)) / 2) x 1 or: Find out how many seconds there are in an hour. Divide that by two then add the quotient back to the number of seconds in one hour. Divide the sum by two to get the number of 2-second intervals there are in an hour-and-a-half. Multiply by the number of words per 2-second interval.

Answer: 2700 words or sound effects

Tips for Modifying: For an easier problem, give all times in the same unit or lose the half-hour. For a harder problem, increase the number of words/sounds per interval.

75.

Difficulty: Easy-Moderate

Skills Needed: subtraction, logical reasoning, even/odd

Problem: The low and the high temperatures in one day were both odd numbers. Does that mean that the change in temperature was an even number or an odd number? Prove it.

Steps: Choose two odd numbers. Subtract them. See if the result is even or odd.

Answer: Even. Subtract several sets of odd numbers. The answer is always even.

Tips for Modifying: For an easier problem, provide actual numbers in the problem.

76.

Difficulty: Easy-Moderate

Skills Needed: division, dealing with remainders

Basic Math

Problem: Bo Urd does bizarre things like perforate paper. He can make 43 holes per minute. How many minutes will it take for him to make at least 623 holes?
Steps: 623 holes / 43 holes/min Round the fraction as needed or provide the number of seconds. To do that, you'll find the percentage of holes the remainder is of the total. In this case, that's 21 out of 43 or .49. Multiply .49 by 60 seconds. That gets you 29 seconds.
Answer: 15 minutes or about 14 minutes, 29 seconds.
Tips for Modifying: For an easier problem, use smaller, more-compatible numbers. For a harder problem, use larger numbers or require a conversion of time units.

77.
Difficulty: Easy-Moderate
Skills Needed: division, subtraction, translating words to numbers
Problem: Dewey Kair has eighty-four thousand bottle caps in his collection. Every year, he collected twelve thousand new ones. If Dewey is fifteen years old now, when did he start collecting?
Steps: 15 years old - (84,000 bottle caps / 12,000 bottle caps/yr)
Answer: 8 yrs old
Tips for Modifying: For an easier problem, use numbers with fewer zeroes or give all numbers in standard number form. For a harder problem, use less-compatible numbers or throw in other odd details like a relative who gives him X bottle caps every year.

78.
Difficulty: Easy-Moderate
Skills Needed: addition, multiplication, translating words to numbers
Problem: Bob Tale keeps rabbits. He has five mini rabbits, ten lop-eared rabbits, and six long-haired rabbits. How many total rabbit feet are in his rabbit pens?
Steps: (5 mini + 10 lop-ear + 6 long-hair) x 4 ft/rabbit

Answer: 84 feet
Tips for Modifying: For an easier problem, give all numbers in standard number form or use more-compatible numbers. For a harder problem, use larger numbers or provide some unnecessary information, such as the number of guinea pigs he has.

79.
Difficulty: Easy-Moderate
Skills Needed: addition, multiplication, translating words to numbers
Problem: Allie Katt has a whole bunch of cats in her house. She has one poor, little tabby she rescued from the pound. This tabby had been in a fight, and he'd lost an ear. Of her other cats, six of them are orange, four of them are gray, two of them are black, and one of them is white. How many total cat ears are in the house?
Steps: ((6 orange + 4 gray + 2 black + 1 white) x 2 ears/cat) + 1 ear on the pound kitty
Answer: 27 ears
Tips for Modifying: For an easier problem, give all numbers in standard number form, take out the business about the one-eared cat, or reduce the number of cat types. For a harder problem, increase the number of cat types or use larger numbers.

80.
Difficulty: Easy-Moderate
Skills Needed: division, eliminating useless data, translating words to numbers
Problem: Kitty Katt went into business walking cats around the neighborhood. She has fifty regular customers. Forty of them are short-haired cats. The rest are long-haired. If she makes an average of $1000.00 every month, how much does she charge for cat-walking?
Steps: $1000/mo / 50 cats The cat types are irrelevant.
Answer: $20/month
Tips for Modifying: For an easier problem, give all numbers in standard number form or get rid of the

Basic Math

useless information. For a harder problem, make the numbers less compatible or add cents to the dollar amounts.

81.
Difficulty: Easy-Moderate
Skills Needed: division, number of days in a week, what to do with remainders, comparing numbers, translating words to numbers
Problem: Kat Toiz has a very finicky cat named Phydeaux. Phydeaux will only play with one kind of toy, and he tends to destroy it every four days. The toy costs $5. If Kat can make $10 per week by cleaning up the kitchen every night, can she make enough to keep Phydeaux supplied with his favorite toy?
Steps: 7 days/wk / 4 days/toy Round remainders up. 2 toys/wk x $5/toy Compare to the amount of money Kat can make in a week.
Answer: Yes.
Tips for Modifying: For an easier problem, make the numbers more compatible or give all numbers in standard number form. For a harder problem, add some cents to the money amounts or rearrange the time it takes for the cat to destroy the toy and the timing of Kat's paycheck.

82.
Difficulty: Easy-Moderate
Skills Needed: division, comparing numbers. This can also be done as a comparing fractions problem.
Problem: Mai Dawg's poodle has fleas. Mai needs to go get some flea soap, but she can't afford a whole lot. She finds a 4 oz bottle for $5 and an 8 oz bottle for $7. Which is a better buy?
Steps: ($5 / 4oz) and ($7 / 8 oz) Compare the results.
Answer: The 8 oz bottle is cheaper per ounce.
Tips for Modifying: For an easier problem, make the numbers more compatible. For a harder problem, increase the number of options.

83.
Difficulty: Easy-Moderate
Skills Needed: multiplication
Problem: A new shop called Puppy Love has opened up for people who want to play with puppies without taking them home. For the cost of $10 per hour, you can play with a puppy by yourself. The shop has 15 puppies right now. What is the maximum amount of money they can make in one 8-hour day?
Steps: ($10/hr x 8 hr/day) x 15 puppies
Answer: $1200
Tips for Modifying: For an easier problem, make the numbers smaller or more compatible so they use basic multiplication facts. For a harder problem, add cents to the dollar amount or use less-compatible numbers. You can also add additional information such as the cost for you and a friend to play with a puppy for an hour.

84.
Difficulty: Easy-Moderate
Skills Needed: multiplication, logical reasoning, addition, translating words to numbers
Problem: Jewel Ree has five bracelets. She has a kit that allows her to make ten times that many. How many will she have when she's finished making bracelets?
Steps: (5 x 10) + 5
Answer: 55
Tips for Modifying: For an easier problem, give all numbers in standard number form. For a harder problem, use less compatible or larger numbers. Introduce extraneous information like the number of rings or necklaces she has.

85.
Difficulty: Easy-Moderate
Skills Needed: multiplication, division
Problem: Bob L. Hedd is collecting bobble head pets. He found a bunch on sale at Wally World for $2 each. For his birthday, he got $5 from each of 6 relatives. If he

Basic Math

spends all his birthday money on bobble head pets, how many will he be able to get?
Steps: ($5/relative x 6 relatives) / $2/bobble head
Answer: 15 bobble heads
Tips for Modifying: For an easier problem, give the total amount of money from his relatives. For a harder problem, include cents in the money amounts or make the number larger.

86.
Difficulty: Easy-Moderate
Skills Needed: addition, multiplication
Problem: Every year his birds molt. Moe Ult gets 58 feathers from Dot and 82 feathers from Huey. After 4 years, how many feathers does Moe have from those two?
Steps: (58 + 82) x 4 yrs
Answer: 560 feathers
Tips for Modifying: For an easier problem, use smaller or more-compatible numbers. For a harder problem, use larger numbers, more birds, or divide the feathers into groups by color or size and only count certain types toward the total.

87.
Difficulty: Easy-Moderate
Skills Needed: addition, multiplication, translating words to numbers
Problem: Penny Earned has written eight novels. Each one is about ninety-thousand words long. She has also written one hundred seventy-two stories. The length varies, but the average length is about thirty-thousand words. How many total words has she written in her novels and stories?
Steps: (90,000 words/novel x 8 novels) + (172 stories x 30,000 words/story)
Answer: 5,880,000 words
Tips for Modifying: For an easier problem, give all numbers in standard number form or use smaller, more-

compatible numbers. For a harder problem, use large numbers with fewer zeroes.

88.
Difficulty: Easy-Moderate
Skills Needed: addition, multiplication, translating words to numbers
Problem: There are one hundred sixty adult novels and seventy-two kid novels in some boxes. The average adult novel is about three hundred pages long. The average kid novel is one hundred fifty pages long. About how many pages of novels are in the boxes?
Steps: (160 novels x 300 pages/novel) + (72 kid novels x 150 pages/kid novel)
Answer: 58,800 pages
Tips for Modifying: For an easier problem, use smaller or more-compatible numbers. For a harder problem, further divide the novels into groups (mysteries, westerns, sci-fi, etc) and give each a different page count. You could also give the average number of words per page and turn the question into "How many words are there?"

89.
Difficulty: Easy-Moderate
Skills Needed: addition, multiplication, translating words to numbers
Problem: Jewel Urr is making a bunch of jewelry for herself and seven of her favorite friends. Each person gets a necklace made of fifteen blue beads, five red beads, and seventy green beads. Each person also gets a bracelet made of six blue beads, one red bead, and fourteen green beads. How many total beads will she need?
Steps: (15 blue + 5 red + 70 green + 6 blue + 1 red + 14 green) x (7 friends + 1 Jewel)
Answer: 888 beads
Tips for Modifying: For an easier problem, use smaller numbers or reduce the number of colors or give the total beads for a necklace and a bracelet. For a

harder problem, use larger numbers or vary how many necklaces and bracelets will be made. You can also change the question to ask how many of one or two particular types of bead will be needed.

90.
Difficulty: Easy-Moderate
Skills Needed: multiplication, conversion of time units
Problem: Harry Dawg takes 58 seconds to do his hair in the morning. Bea Quick takes 10 times as long as Harry to do her hair. How many minutes does it take Bea to do her hair in the morning?
Steps: (58 seconds x 10 times as long) / 60 seconds/minute
Answer: 9 minutes, 40 seconds
Tips for Modifying: For an easier problem, use more-compatible numbers. For a harder problem, use larger numbers or numbers that don't end with zero. You can also change the question to ask how much time she needs to do her hair each week.

91.
Difficulty: Easy-Moderate
Skills Needed: division, multiplication, translating words to numbers, converting time units, comparing numbers
Problem: Annie Versary and Bert Day are going head to head in Around the World. Annie can answer one multiplication problem every two seconds. Bert can answer thirty-one problems in one minute. Who is most likely to win the round?
Steps: (60 sec/min / 2 sec per problem) x 1 problem
Compare to the number he can do in one minute. The highest one is most likely to win.
Answer: Bert wins, barely.
Tips for Modifying: For an easier problem, give all numbers in standard number form. For a harder problem, toss in a third person or give Bert's speed in a different number of seconds (like 3 problems in 4 seconds).

92.
Difficulty: Moderate
Skills Needed: addition, multiplication
Problem: Martina, a gray and yellow cockatiel, likes to wear her bell for a hat. Each time she does, she wears her hat for 5 minutes. On Monday, she does that 4 times. On Tuesday, she does that 19 times. On Wednesday, she does that 83 times. On Thursday, she does that 13 times. On Friday, she goes all out and does that 90 times. How many minutes every week does she spend wearing her bell like a hat?
Steps: 5 min/time x (4 times + 19 times + 83 times + 13 times + 90 times)
Answer: 1045 minutes
Tips for Modifying: For an easier problem, use smaller or more-compatible numbers. For a harder problem, give the time in minutes and require the answer in hours or seconds.

93.
Difficulty: Moderate
Skills Needed: multiplication, logical reasoning, fact families, counting
Problem: Rex Cars must make multiplication flashcards, but he doesn't want to make more than he absolutely has to. He decided to eliminate ones that are duplicates because they're in the same fact family. If he does only one in a fact family, how many does he have to do? (use numerals 1-12)
Steps: Make a multiplication chart. Color the diagonal line representing all the squares. Cross off everything below that diagonal. Count the diagonal and everything above it.
Answer: 78
Tips for Modifying: For an easier problem, provide a multiplication chart already filled in.

94.

Basic Math

Difficulty: Moderate
Skills Needed: addition, fact families, logical reasoning, counting
Problem: Rose Bush has to make addition flashcards, but she doesn't want to make more than she absolutely has to. She decided to eliminate ones that are duplicates because they're in the same fact family. If she does only one in a fact family, how many does she have to do?
Steps: Make an addition chart. Color in the diagonal line for all the doubles. Cross out anything below that line. Count the doubles line and everything above it. (use numerals 1-10)
Answer: 55
Tips for Modifying: For an easier problem, provide an addition chart already filled in.

95.
Difficulty: Moderate
Skills Needed: multiplication, division, subtraction
Problem: Jan bought 7 pies and 4 cakes. The pies cost $8 each. The cakes cost half as much. How much change will Jan get back from a $100 bill?
Steps: 100 - ((7 pies x $8/pie) + (($8/pie / 2) x 4 cakes))
Multiply pies by the cost per pie. Cut the cost per pie in half and multiply by the number of cakes. Add those two together. Subtract from 100.
Answer: $28
Tips for Modifying: For an easier problem, provide the cost of a pie or ask for the total amount of money needed rather than the change back from a $100 bill. For a harder problem, use numbers that aren't basic multiplication facts or include cents in the costs.

96.
Difficulty: Moderate
Skills Needed: multiplication, addition, translating numbers to words
Problem: In 1870 the population of Texas was 818,579. If the population grew by 2,000 every year since 1870,

what is the population now? Write the new population in words.
Steps: Subtract the current year and 1870. Multiply by 2000. Add the result to the population in 1870.
For example, in 2012, that would look like this:
((2012 - 1870) x 2000) + 818,579
Answer: 1,102,579 or one million, one hundred two thousand, five hundred seventy-nine
Tips for Modifying: For an easier problem, give the 1870 population in a number with lots of zeroes at the end or move the date up closer to the current one. For a harder problem, increase the population growth or give the population growth in terms of multiple years, such as 15,843 per five years.

97.
Difficulty: Moderate
Skills Needed: division, addition, translating words to numbers
Problem: Someone donated the weirdest dogs to a local fire station. They were all dalmatians, and although they weren't identical, they all had the same number of spots. Altogether, there were eighteen large spots, twenty-seven medium-sized spots, and fifty-four small spots. If there are three dogs, how many spots are on each dog?
Steps: (18 + 27 + 54) / 3
Answer: 33 spots
Tips for Modifying: For an easier problem, give all numbers in standard number form. For a harder problem, use larger numbers or include some useless information, preferably something with a number attached.

98.
Difficulty: Moderate
Skills Needed: multiplication, subtraction, division
Problem: Shaw Perr bought 5 ties and 4 shirts for his dad. Each shirt cost $15. The total cost for all the shirts and ties was $100. How much did each tie cost?
Steps: ($100 - (4 shirts x $15/shirt)) / 5 ties

Basic Math

Answer: $8
Tips for Modifying: For an easier problem, take out the cost per shirt and the number of ties or use a smaller shirt cost. For a harder problem, add cents to the dollar amounts. Add some useless information like the number of pairs of pants or how much a pair of shoes cost.

99.
Difficulty: Moderate
Skills Needed: multiplication, addition
Problem: Kay Bull is going to get cable internet for Christmas. If the set up charge is $99 and the cost per month is $35, what will be the cost for the first year of cable internet?
Steps: ($35/month x 12 months) + $99 setup fee
Answer: $519
Tips for Modifying: For an easier problem, use smaller numbers or eliminate the extra set up charge. For a harder problem, add cents to the charges or increase the number of years. You can also make this about setting money aside to pay for it. Give an amount set aside, say $500, and ask if that'll be enough to cover it.

100.
Difficulty: Moderate
Skills Needed: multiplication, division, translating words to numbers, time measurement conversions
Problem: Mike Ees's dachshund sleeps a lot. She sleeps for two minutes out of every five in the day. How many hours does Mike's dog sleep in one day?
Steps: (60min/hr / 5 min) x 2 min x 24 hr/day / 60 min/hr
Divide five minutes into one hour to get the number of sets of five minutes there are. Multiply that by the number of minutes the dog sleeps. Multiply by 24 hours in one day. Divide by 60 minutes to the hour.
Answer: 9 hours 36 minutes
Tips for Modifying: For an easier problem, use more-compatible numbers or put the numbers in standard

number form. For a harder problem, change the question to the number of hours the dog sleeps in a week.

101.
Difficulty: Moderate
Skills Needed: recognizing the number of days per month, multiplication, translating words to numbers
Problem: Peter Piper picks pecks of pickled peppers. If Peter Piper picks seven pecks of pickled peppers every day, how many pecks of pickled peppers will Peter Piper pick in the month of September? (He does not get days off.)
Steps: 7 pecks/day x 30 days/September
Answer: 210 pecks of peppers in September
Tips for Modifying: For an easier problem, take out the tongue twister part, provide the number of days in September, or use smaller numbers. For a harder problem, use larger or fractional numbers or give Peter some number days off expressed in a ratio such as one day in four.

102.
Difficulty: Moderate
Skills Needed: time conversions, multiplication, translating words to numbers
Problem: If a canner can can cans, I suspect that a canner can can cans at the rate of ten cans per hour. If I employ a canner to can cans for three eight-hour days, how many cans can a canner can if a canner can can cans?
Steps: 10 cans/hr x 8 hrs/day x 3 days
Answer: 240 cans
Tips for Modifying: For an easier problem, rephrase the question to get rid of the tongue twister For a harder problem, make the numbers larger or less compatible.

103.
Difficulty: Moderate
Skills Needed: prime vs. composite, multiplication

Basic Math

Problem: What is the product of the first 4 prime numbers?
Steps: 2 x 3 x 5 x 7
Answer: 210
Tips for Modifying: For an easier problem, provide a chart of prime and composite numbers or reduce the number of primes needed. You can also change the operation to a sum. For a harder problem, increase the number of primes needed. This kind of problem also works with composite numbers.

104.
Difficulty: Moderate
Skills Needed: multiplication, days per week
Problem: Kanya Seeyit does jumping jacks every day during recess. She can do 30 jumping jacks per minute. Recess is 30 minutes long. How many jumping jacks does Kanya do in one week?
Steps: 30 jumping jacks/min x 30 min/recess x 5 days/school week
Answer: 4500 jumping jacks in a 5-day school week.
Tips for Modifying: For an easier problem, use smaller numbers or stop at finding out the number of jumping jacks in one recess. For a harder problem, use less-compatible numbers.

105.
Difficulty: Moderate
Skills Needed: multiplication, addition, days per year, weeks per year, subtracting
Problem: Dee Side and Mai Sandmen are having a contest to see who can collect the most bird stamps in one year. Dee buys 5 stamps every week with his allowance. For Dee's birthday, he received 26 bird stamps from his grandma. Mai's dad works in a store that sells old stamps. He brings her one new bird stamp every day. At the end of the year, who wins by how much?
Steps: Dee = (5 stamps/wk x 52 wks/yr) + 26 stamps from grandma

Mai = 1 stamp/day x 365 days
Subtract Mai's and Dee's stamp collection sizes.
Answer: Dee gets 286 stamps. Mai gets 365 stamps. Mai wins by 79 stamps.
Tips for Modifying: For an easier problem, take out the number of stamps Dee gets from his grandma or use more-compatible numbers. For a harder problem, use larger numbers or change the intervals that Dee and Mai receive stamps.

106.
Difficulty: Moderate
Skills Needed: multiplication, comparing numbers, translating words to numbers
Problem: Jim Nasium is starting a new exercise program. His doctor recommended he get a minimum of one hundred fifty minutes of exercise every week. He signed up for a program that lets him work out at the gym for thirty-five minutes a day, four days a week. Will he meet the goal his doctor set?
Steps: 35 min/day x 4 days Compare that to 150 minutes
Answer: No. He comes 10 minutes short.
Tips for Modifying: For an easier problem, give the numbers in standard number form or use smaller, more-compatible numbers. For a harder problem, use larger numbers or introduce fractions to the times. You can also vary the amount of time he spends on exercise each day.

107.
Difficulty: Moderate
Skills Needed: multiplication, translating words to numbers, weeks per year
Problem: Harry Beast has eight dogs. Each dog eats ten pounds of dog food every week. How much food will Harry need to feed his dogs for one year?
Steps: 8 dogs x 10 pounds/wk x 52 wks/yr
Answer: 4160 pounds of dog food

Basic Math

Tips for Modifying: For an easier problem, give all numbers in standard number form or use smaller numbers. For a harder problem, use larger numbers or increase the number of years or require the answer in tons or ounces.

108.
Difficulty: Moderate
Skills Needed: division, days in a week, dealing with remainders
Problem: P. Yourblud has heard about a new breed of dog called a Canardly. He simply must get one for his dog collection. Canardlies cost $2000. If Mr. Yourblud can save $15 per week, how many days before he can get his Canardly?
Steps: ($2000/Canardly / $15/wk) x 7 days/wk Round any remainders up.
Answer: 934 days if you round at the end or 938 days if you round immediately after dividing
Tips for Modifying: For an easier problem, make the numbers more compatible or take out the unit conversion for the answer. For a harder problem, introduce other information such as an amount of money already saved or other sources of income.

109.
Difficulty: Moderate
Skills Needed: division, multiplication, addition, translating words to numbers
Problem: To make a large gourd shaker, Gordon Mihand needs seventy-two shells. To make a small gourd shaker, he needs half as many shells as the large gourd shaker. He needs to make two large gourd shakers and three small gourd shakers. How many shells will he need altogether?
Steps: (72 shells/large shaker x 2 large shakers) + ((72 shells/large shaker) / 2) x 3 shakers)
Answer: 252 shells
Tips for Modifying: For an easier problem, give all numbers in standard number form or use smaller

numbers. For a harder problem, use larger or less-compatible numbers. You can also change the number of shells by requiring different numbers of different types of shells such as 50 round shells and 25 flat ones for one shaker.

110.
Difficulty: Moderate
Skills Needed: multiplication, addition
Problem: Jim Nasium drives 30 miles to work every morning. On Monday evenings, he drives the same distance home. On Tuesdays, he needs to drive an additional 5 miles to go to the store. On Wednesdays and Thursdays, he goes an additional 16 miles to pick up his friend from work. On Fridays, he takes a different route home to avoid traffic. That route is 38 miles long. In 5 days, how many total miles does he drive?
Steps: (30 miles x 5 days) + (30 miles x 4 days) + 5 miles + (16 miles x 2 days) + 38 miles **Answer:** 345 miles
Tips for Modifying: For an easier problem, use smaller numbers or simplify the miles for the trip home by saying he drives the same distance home every day. For a harder problem, use larger numbers or make some days a function of other days like on Wednesday, he drives three times as far in extra miles as he did on Tuesday.

111.
Difficulty: Moderate
Skills Needed: multiplication, translating words to numbers
Problem: Susie sells seashells by the seashore. If Susie sells seventy seashells by the seashore every Sunday afternoon for sixty-seven weeks, how many seashells does Susie sell by the seashore?
Steps: 70 shells x 67 weeks
Answer: 4690 shells
Tips for Modifying: For an easier problem, use easier or more-compatible numbers or give the numbers in

Basic Math

standard number form. For a harder problem, divide the shells up by type and give different numbers for each or include the cost per shell and find out how much money she made.

112.
Difficulty: Moderate-Hard
Skills Needed: addition, division, multiplication, translating words to numbers
Problem: Priddy Messay has eight dresses. Four are pink, two are yellow, and the rest are blue. After playing outside all week, they're all so dirty you can't tell what color they are any more. Getting them cleaned cost Priddy's mom a total of $64 dollars. All the dresses cost the same amount to clean. What is the cost for cleaning just the blue ones
Steps: ($64 / (4 pink + 2 yellow + (8 total dresses - 4 pink - 2 yellow))) x (8 total dresses - 4 pink - 2 yellow)
Add up the numbers of dresses for the colors given. Subtract from 8 to get the number of blue dresses. Divide the total cost by the number of dresses. Multiply that by the number of blue dresses.
Answer: $16
Tips for Modifying: For an easier problem, give all numbers in standard number form or reduce the number of colors. For a harder problem, use numbers that are less compatible or include cents in the total cost. You can also ask for the cost for each color individually.

113.
Difficulty: Moderate-Hard
Skills Needed: converting time measurements, multiplication, comparing numbers
Problem: Burt Luvre has three parrots. Kritter and Gooberhead got into a bell-ringing contest. Kritter can ring his bell 15 times in 5 seconds. Gooberhead can ring his 100 times in one minute. Meanwhile, Squawker just looked at them both like they were crazy. Who rings their bell the most in one hour?

Steps: Kritter = ((60 sec/min / 5 sec) x 15) x 60 min/hr
Gooberhead = 100 times/min x 60 min/hr
Answer: Kritter rings his bell the most in one hour.
Tips for Modifying: For an easier problem, remove some of the conversions. Give all times for the birds in terms of one minute. For a harder problem, give the third bird some number of times to ring the bell, preferably not in the same terms as the other two. Use numbers that are less compatible.

114.
Difficulty: Moderate-Hard
Skills Needed: converting time measurements, multiplication, division
Problem: If a woodchuck could chuck wood, I suspect a woodchuck would chuck 5 pieces of wood every ten minutes. If I employ a woodchuck to chuck wood for forty hours, how much wood would a woodchuck chuck if a woodchuck could chuck wood?
Steps: 60 min/hr / 10 min x 5 pieces x 40 hours
Answer: 1200 pieces chucked
Tips for Modifying: For an easier problem, use smaller numbers. For a harder problem, use numbers that are less compatible.

115.
Difficulty: Moderate-Hard
Skills Needed: multiplication, addition, translating words to numbers
Problem: There are fifteen elephants in a parade. Each elephant is carrying two riders. Each rider has two dogs in his arms. How many legs are there in the parade?
Steps: (15 elephants x 4 legs/elephant) + (2 riders/elephant x 2 legs/rider x 15 elephants) + (2 dogs/rider x 2 riders/elephant x 4 legs/dog x 15 elephants)
Multiply elephants by the number of legs on an elephant. Multiply riders by the number of legs on a rider then by the number of elephants. Multiply dogs per rider by the number of riders per elephant then by the number of

Basic Math

legs per dog then by the number of elephants. Add all products.
Alternately, it's helpful to draw an elephant with all the stuff on the elephant, count the legs and multiply by the number of elephants.
Answer: 360 legs
Tips for Modifying: For an easier problem, give all numbers in standard number form or use smaller, more-compatible numbers. You can also reduce the number of people or critters riding on an elephant. For a harder problem, use larger numbers.

116.
Difficulty: Moderate-Hard
Skills Needed: multiplication, subtraction, translating words to numbers
Problem: Grey Bird collects feathers to make into hats. He needs five hundred feathers for one hat. He has one hat already and orders for a total of five hats. How many more feathers does he need?
Steps: (5 hats ordered - 1 hat completed) x 500 feathers/hat
Answer: 2000 feathers
Tips for Modifying: For an easier problem, give numbers in standard number form or use smaller numbers. For a harder problem, use less-compatible numbers. You can also provide the number of feathers he has on hand and ask how many he still needs to collect.

117.
Difficulty: Moderate-Hard
Skills Needed: multiplication, dealing with fractions and decimals, unit conversions, comparing numbers
Problem: Huey Yupp made 2 bags for his mom to carry groceries in. The material cost $1 per yard. Huey needed 3 1/2 feet to make the bags. How much material did Huey have to buy? How much did it cost? When Huey went to the store later that week, he found the same kind

of bag on sale for $5 each. Did he save money by making the bags himself?
Steps: (2 bags x 3 1/2 feet/bag) / 3ft/yd x $1/yd
Compare this to the cost for the bags he made.
Answer: Amount of material to buy = 7' or 2 1/3 yards or 3 yards if you round up fractions. Cost for the bags = $2.33 for 2 1/3 yards or $3 for 3 yards, Cost of bags at the store = $10, so he saved a lot of money.
Tips for Modifying: For an easier problem, make the numbers more compatible and get rid of the fractions. For a harder problem, make the numbers larger or include cents in the money amounts.

118.
Difficulty: Moderate-Hard
Skills Needed: addition, division, translating words to numbers, dealing with remainders
Problem: There are fifteen bags of fruit on the shelf. Each bag contains four apples, five oranges, three grapefruits, and ninety-six grapes. There are twenty kids in the class. If the teacher divided all the fruit evenly among the students, how many pieces does each person get?
Steps: (5 oranges + 4 apples + 3 grapefruits + 96 grapes) x 15 bags / 20 kids/class
Answer: 81 pieces per kid.
Tips for Modifying: For an easier problem, give all numbers in standard number form or use smaller numbers or fewer kinds of fruit. You can also use only one bag of fruit. For a harder problem, use larger numbers or set up some kind of equivalency system where one grapefruit equals 2 oranges.

119.
Difficulty: Moderate-Hard
Skills Needed: division with decimals in the answer, comparing numbers
Problem: Sam Yule is in a race with his sister to see who can finish their math homework first. She has 25 problems to do. He has 38 of his own problems to do. In

Basic Math

the time it takes for her to answer 2 problems, he can answer 3. Who will win?
Steps: Sister = 25/2
Sam = 38/3
The one with the lowest answer wins. This might be easier for some to solve using a diagram.
Answer: She wins, but just barely.
Tips for Modifying: For an easier problem, use more-compatible numbers so there aren't remainders. For a harder problem, use larger numbers or give actual times that it takes from them to complete 2 or 3 problems respectively. To make it even harder, use different times for each, such as she does 2 problems in four minutes while he does 3 problems in five minutes.

120.
Difficulty: Moderate-Hard
Skills Needed: multiplication, addition, division
Problem: Bonnie Rabutt and Ken Null decide to go into business together. Bonnie is going to open a new rabbit-sitter service, and Ken will provide the happy bunnies with entertainment by doing Charlie Chaplin impersonations. Food is going to cost them $50 per month. They each want to make $25 per month. If Bonnie's rabbit cages can hold 10 rabbits, what is the least amount of money they should charge for rabbit-sitting every month?
Steps: (($25/person x 2 people) + $50 for food) / 10 rabbits
Answer: $10 per rabbit
Tips for Modifying: For an easier problem, use smaller numbers. For a harder problem, use numbers that are less compatible or include cents in the dollar amounts.

Decimals

121.
Difficulty: Easy
Skills Needed: adding decimals
Problem: There's a new restaurant in town called Three Dog Nite. People can go out to eat and take their dogs with them. Dog food costs the restaurant $.84 per plate. How much are they charging if they make $5.12 in profits for each plate of dog food?
Steps: $.84 + $5.12
Answer: $5.96
Tips for Modifying: For an easier problem, use whole dollar amounts. For a harder problem, add in sales tax.

122.
Difficulty: Easy-Moderate
Skills Needed: translating words to numbers, addition of decimals, comparing numbers
Problem: Allie Jence bought seven and eight tenths meters of material for a dress. When Allie got home, she changed her mind and decided to make a shirt and a skirt. The shirt takes three and fifty-two hundredths of a meter of material. The skirt takes four and two hundredths of a meter of material. Does she have enough material?
Steps: 3.52 + 4.02 Compare to 7.8
Answer: Yes, there's enough.
Tips for Modifying: For an easier problem, give all numbers in standard number form or use more-compatible numbers. For a harder problem, use decimals to the thousandths.

123.
Difficulty: Easy-Moderate
Skills Needed: multiplying and adding decimals, translating words to numbers
Problem: Abby Normal is buying everything she can find in a craft store that costs less than a dollar. She

Basic Math

bought six things that cost fifty cents each, five things that cost forty cents each, and thirteen things that cost two for fifty cents. How much money did she spend?
Steps: (6 x $.50) + (5 x $.40) + ((13/2) x $.50)
Answer: $8.25
Tips for Modifying: For an easier problem, get rid of the two for fifty cents part or give all numbers in standard number form. For a harder problem, increase the number of objects purchased or include some things that were on sale for half off.

124.
Difficulty: Easy-Moderate
Skills Needed: multiplying by decimals, translating words to numbers
Problem: Chu Yerfood and five friends met for dinner last night. Each of them paid fifteen dollars and ten cents for dinner. How much money did they spend altogether?
Steps: (5 + 1) x $15.10
Answer: $90.60
Tips for Modifying: For an easier problem, make all money values in even dollars or give all numbers in standard number form. For a harder problem, add information about how much their sodas and desserts were.

125.
Difficulty: Easy-Moderate
Skills Needed: adding and subtracting decimals
Problem: Mac N. Cheese is making a lunch run to a McD's this afternoon. After he takes everyone's order, Ms. Understand gives him $10. Ms. Demeanor gives him $5. Ms. Begotten gives him $15. Ms. Turry gives him $3. Mac didn't order anything at McD's. The total cost was $27.46. How much money did the clerk give back to Mac?
Steps: ($10 + $5 + $15 + $3) - $27.46
Answer: $5.54
Tips for Modifying: For an easier problem, get rid of the cents in the total cost. For a harder problem, add

cents to the amounts of money given to Mac or make some of the amounts a factor of some others, like Ms. Understand gave him twice as much as Ms. Demeanor.

126.
Difficulty: Easy-Moderate
Skills Needed: division of decimals, multiplication
Problem: Bill Offgoods has a collection of comic books. Every week, he gets an allowance of $15 because he does a lot of chores around the house and keeps his grades up. Comic books cost $2.95 each. How many comic books can he get each month (4 weeks)?
Steps: ($15 x 4) / $2.95 Ignore remainders
Answer: 20 comic books
Tips for Modifying: For an easier problem, problem, use whole dollar amounts. For a harder problem, give Bill's list of chores and what he earns for each one each week as well as what he gets for his grades.

127.
Difficulty: Moderate
Skills Needed: division by decimal, dealing with remainders
Problem: Gerry Rigged has a huge pen. The pen holds 43 mL of ink. If Gerry uses .33 mL of ink every day, how many full days will his pen last?
Steps: 43mL / .33mL. Drop the remainders.
Answer: 130 days
Tips for Modifying: For an easier problem, use compatible numbers or get rid of the decimal. For a harder problem, give him different amounts of ink to use every day.

128.
Difficulty: Moderate
Skills Needed: translating words to numbers, adding and subtracting decimals
Problem: Lucky Kidd has nineteen dollars and ninety-eight cents. He paid five dollars and eight cents for a ceramic bird. Then he paid twelve dollars and seventy-

Basic Math

two cents for a used CD by Kansas. Next, he found his friend, who paid him back the seven dollars and fifty-three cents she owed him. So, he went to lunch and paid six dollars and forty-seven cents for salad. How much money does Lucky have left?
Steps: $19.98 - $5.08 - $12.72 + $7.53 - $6.47
Answer: $3.24
Tips for Modifying: For an easier problem, give all numbers in standard number form or remove some of the items or lose all the cents or round the cents to the nearest quarter. For a harder problem, make some things a factor of other things. For example, the CD was twice as much as the ceramic bird.

129.
Difficulty: Moderate
Skills Needed: adding and subtracting decimals, translating words to numbers, multiplication, coin amounts, converting cents to dollars
Problem: Dolly Haus got some money for her birthday. As a joke, everyone gave her coins. Her aunt gave her five nickels and twenty dimes. Her sister gave her five dimes and twenty nickels. Her brother gave her five hundred pennies. Then Dolly went out to buy a toy that cost four dollars and ninety-eight cents and some gum for seventy-five cents. How much money does she have left?
Steps: ((5 x $.05) + (20 x $.10) + (5 x $.10) + (20 x .05) + (500 x $.01)) - $4.98 - $.75
Answer: $3.02
Tips for Modifying: For an easier problem, give the value of the gifts in only one kind of coin or give all numbers in standard number form. For a harder problem, include more coins in different amounts and more objects that she bought.

130.
Difficulty: Moderate
Skills Needed: multiplication by decimals, comparing numbers

Problem: Jack Squat can use either hairspray or gel to make his hair spike in front. Hairspray costs $0.09 per ounce, and each time he does his hair, he uses .75 ounces if he uses hairspray. Gel costs $0.05 per ounce, and each time he does his hair, he uses 2.2 ounces if he uses gel. Which would cost him the least to use per day?
Steps: Compare ($.09 x .75) to ($.05 x 2.2) The lowest result wins.
Answer: Hairspray
Tips for Modifying: For an easier problem, express the money as cents rather than dollars and make the number of ounces a whole number. For a harder problem, include some extraneous information or include a third set of information.

131.
Difficulty: Moderate
Skills Needed: multiplying and adding decimals, value of coins, comparing numbers
Problem: Gummy Wurms went to a candy store to get a snack. He picked up a pack of jellybeans for $3.12 and a pack of sour apples for $2.98. He has 52 quarters in his wallet. Does he have enough to pay for the candy?
Steps: (52 x $.25) - ($3.12 + $2.98)
Answer: Yes, he has plenty.
Tips for Modifying: For an easier problem, give the amount of money in whole dollars. For a harder problem, increase the types of coins he has or the number of things he buys.

132.
Difficulty: Moderate
Skills Needed: multiplication, subtracting decimals
Problem: Dov Coat is saving up his money to buy a new jacket with the name of his favorite football team on it. The jacket will cost him $193.73. He mowed 7 yards over the summer for $20 each. How much money does he still need to get?
Steps: $193.73 - (7 x $20)
Answer: $53.73

Basic Math

Tips for Modifying: For an easier problem, give the amount of money he earned over the summer or drop the cents for the jacket cost. For a harder problem, add cents to the cost for yard-mowing or list additional things he either bought or did to earn money.

133.
Difficulty: Moderate
Skills Needed: adding and multiplying decimals
Problem: Stu Meet is cooking dinner for eighteen of his closest friends. Each person's dinner cost $5.31 for the meat, $8.32 dollars for the vegetables, and $2.39 for dessert. How much did Stu spend for dinner for himself and his friends?
Steps: ($5.31 + $8.32 + 2.39) x (18 + 1 for Stu)
Answer: $304.38
Tips for Modifying: For an easier problem, make all dollar amounts even or rounded to the nearest quarter. For a harder problem, add in more things for dinner or make some things a factor of something else, such as the cost of vegetables was four times the cost of dessert.

134.
Difficulty: Moderate
Skills Needed: adding and multiplying decimals
Problem: Amaya Hayr got some new hair jewelry. She picked up 2 sets of hair picks for $1.99 each, and five beaded hair scrunchies for $3.20 each. What was the total cost for her new hair jewelry?
Steps: (2 x $1.99) + (5 x $3.20)
Answer: $19.98
Tips for Modifying: For an easier problem, give all money values in whole dollars. For a harder problem, provide the amount of money she had in her pocket and ask for the amount of change she has left.

135.
Difficulty: Moderate
Skills Needed: multiplying by decimals, dividing a decimal number

Cindy Koepp

Problem: Drew Pixer is collecting doodles other people have made. He currently has a collection of 48 doodles. Skippy D'Lou offers to pay him $.12 for each of his doodles. How much money would he have if he sold half his doodles?
Steps: 48 / 2 x $.12
Answer: $2.88
Tips for Modifying: For an easier problem, use compatible numbers. For a harder problem, someone else makes a different offer, like $.28 for three doodles. The question becomes which offer should he accept.

136.
Difficulty: Moderate
Skills Needed: comparing numbers, multiplying and adding decimals
Problem: Daisy wants to open a flower shop. She's deciding on the name of the shop. She wants to call it Daisy's Daisies or Oopsie-Daisies. It all comes down to the price of the sign. The sign maker charges $4.83 for each letter that has curves and $9.32 for each letter that has no curves. Punctuation, like apostrophes and hyphens will cost $2.48 each. Which sign will cost less?
Steps: Daisy's Daisies = (9 curved letters x $4.83) + (4 uncurved letters x $9.32) + $2.48 (43.47 + 37.28 + 2.48 = $83.23)
Oopsie-Daisies = (10 curved letters x $4.83) + (3 uncurved letters x $9.32) + $2.48 (48.30 + 27.96 + 2.48 = $78.74)
Compare the results. The lowest number wins.
Answer: Oopsie-Daisies
Tips for Modifying: For an easier problem, use whole dollar amounts or cents divisible by 10 or 25. For a harder problem, include some unnecessary information or a third sign option.

137.
Difficulty: Moderate
Skills Needed: dividing by decimals

Basic Math

Problem: Moe Tersicle bought an electronic toy for his cat. This toy is a self-propelled motorcycle just like his and has a dangling fuzzball on the back for the cat to chase. The toy cost $28.83. If his allowance is $1.50 a week, how long did it take for him to save the money?
Steps: $28.83 / $1.50 Round all remainders up.
Answer: 20 weeks
Tips for Modifying: For an easier problem, make all money values even dollar amounts. For harder problem, include other things Moe did to earn money or include other things he bought.

138.
Difficulty: Moderate
Skills Needed: multiplying, adding and subtracting decimals
Problem: Burt Sede has $25. He went to the store and bought a toothbrush for $2.13, 12 bananas for $.30 each, a bag of bird seed for $5.32, and a toy for his parrot for $4.86. When he handed the clerk his money, how much did he get back?
Steps: $25 - ((12 bananas x $.30/banana) + $2.13 + $5.32 + $4.86)
Answer: $9.09
Tips for Modifying: For an easier problem, make all dollar amounts even dollars. Give the cost for the bunch of bananas instead of for each banana. For a harder problem, increase the number of each kind of thing Bert bought. Give the money he started with in dollars and cents.

139.
Difficulty: Moderate
Skills Needed: multiplying and adding decimals
Problem: Every month, Ben Kerr manages to save $100.38. In December, he manages to save an additional $2.84. How much money does he save in a year?
Steps: ($100.38 x 12) + $2.84
Answer: $1207.40

Tips for Modifying: For an easier problem, give all dollar amounts in whole dollars. For a harder problem, give Ben something to be saving toward and a dollar amount, like a $2500 vacation to Disney. The question turns into, "Can he save enough money?" or "How long will it take him to save enough money?"

140.
Difficulty: Moderate
Skills Needed: multiplication, converting cents to dollars, comparing numbers
Problem: Sam U. Well and Ari Ull had big dreams of opening their own lemonade stands for the summer. Over the course of the summer, Sam sold 4,829 cups of lemonade for 5 cents per cup. Ari sold 52 gallons of lemonade for $1 per gallon. Who made the most money?
Steps: 4829 x $.05 = Sam
52 x $1 = Ari
Compare the numbers. The biggest one wins.
Answer: Sam won by rather a lot.
Tips for Modifying: For an easier problem, use smaller or more-compatible numbers. For a harder problem, give the amounts they sold in different units than the amount charged. For example, Sam sold 48 gallons of lemonade for 5 cents per cup.

141.
Difficulty: Moderate-Hard
Skills Needed: multiplication and addition of decimals, logical reasoning
Problem: Jose Kanyusee won some money in a shoe-tying contest. To celebrate, he took his mom, dad, and brother out to dinner and a movie. After all was said and done, he had exactly enough money left to buy a CD for $15.93. The movie cost $9 per person. Dinner cost $12.95 per person. How much money did he win in the contest?
Steps: (4 x $9) + (4 x $12.95) + $15.93
Answer: $103.73

Basic Math

Tips for Modifying: For an easier problem, use smaller numbers or eliminate decimals. For a harder problem, use bigger numbers or add more stuff that he bought either for himself or for his family.

142.
Difficulty: Moderate-Hard
Skills Needed: multiplying by decimals, rounding, number of weeks in a year
Problem: Zane Neekid has a weird hobby. He does critter impersonations on stage. Every Saturday, he performs for all his friends. Tickets to his performances cost $0.05. If he averages 10 members of the audience every Saturday, about how much money does he make in one year to the nearest dollar?
Steps: 10 x $.05 x 52 wks/yr
Answer: $26
Tips for Modifying: For an easier problem, express the money in cents rather than dollars. For a harder problem, use less-compatible numbers.

143.
Difficulty: Moderate-Hard
Skills Needed: multiplying and dividing decimals, translating words to numbers
Problem: Billy Gote has sixty-nine matchbox cars. For his birthday, his four friends chip in and buy him more matchbox cars. The cars cost one dollar and forty-nine cents each. If each friend contributed five dollars and forty cents, how many matchbox cars does Billy have after his birthday?
Steps: 69 cars + (($5.40 x 4) / $1.49) drop all remainders
Answer: 83 cars
Tips for Modifying: For an easier problem, get rid of the cents or give all numbers in standard number form. For a harder problem, use larger numbers or have other people contributing different amounts to the money used to buy the cars.

144.
Difficulty: Moderate-Hard
Skills Needed: adding and subtracting decimals, multiplying
Problem: Paige Turner's dad loves the University of Texas. She is playing a trick on her dad for his birthday. She got him a Texas A&M T-shirt, an A&M coffee cup, and an A&M pencil. The shirt cost $21.20. The coffee cup cost $4.27. She got back $2.19 from 3 $10 bills. How much did the pencil cost?
Steps: (3 x $10) - ($21.20 + $4.27 + $2.19)
Answer: $2.34
Tips for Modifying: For an easier problem, use whole dollar amounts or cents in multiples of 10 or 25. You can also reduce the amount of stuff she bought. For a harder problem, make some things the result of an operation of something else. For example, the amount of change she had at the end was half the amount of the coffee cup.

Basic Math

Estimations, Range

Estimation problems are solved by converting the numbers in the problem to either compatible numbers (easily added, subtracted, multiplied, or divided mentally), or rounding each of the components of the problem.

145.
Difficulty: Easy
Skills Needed: rounding, adding
Problem: The wild birds at Willy Feedem's house go through a bunch of seeds, but they always leave the hulls behind. One day, they ate 383 seeds. The second day, they ate 689 seeds. The third day, they ate 384 seeds. To the nearest hundred, how many total seeds did they eat in the three days?
Steps: 400 + 700 + 400
Answer: 1500 seeds
Tips for Modifying: For an easier problem, remove some of the extra story business or use significantly smaller numbers. For a harder problem, use significantly larger numbers or more days.

146.
Difficulty: Easy
Skills Needed: multiplication
Problem: Mai Callangelo became bored over the summer and decided to paint the blades of grass in her yard orange. While painting, she counted 20,000 blades of grass in her front yard. The backyard is twice as large. What is a reasonable estimate for the number of blades of grass in the back yard?
Steps: 20,000 x 2.
Answer: 40,000 blades of grass
Tips for Modifying: For an easier problem, use smaller numbers still divisible by 10 or 100. For a harder problem, use less-compatible numbers or a different ratio between the front and back yard.

147.
Difficulty: Easy
Skills Needed: addition, rounding, translating words to numbers
Problem: Fred got bored one afternoon and counted dust particles in his house. His kitchen had four million, seventeen thousand, thirty-two dust particles. His living room had five hundred fifty-six million, nine hundred two thousand, five hundred fifty dust particles. His bedroom had seven hundred thirty-eight million, four thousand, three hundred two dust particles. To the nearest million, approximately how many dust particles are there in Fred's house?
Steps: 557,000,000 + 738,000,000 + 4,000,000
Answer: 1,299,000,000 dust particles
Tips for Modifying: For an easier problem, use smaller or more-compatible numbers. For a harder problem, make one room a factor of another one, such as the number of particles in the living room is 8 times the number in the bedroom.

148.
Difficulty: Easy
Skills Needed: rounding, division
Problem: Dawg Gonnit has lost his dog. He decides to make full-color posters to put up around town. Each poster costs $1.95 to make. If he has $20, about how many posters can he make?
Steps: $20 / $2
Answer: 10 posters
Tips for Modifying: For an easier problem, use smaller numbers. For a harder problem, use less-compatible numbers.

149.
Difficulty: Easy
Skills Needed: translating words to numbers, rounding or compatible numbers, multiplication
Problem: Ella Gants is going to move soon. She has to pack all of her books into four boxes. Whatever doesn't

Basic Math

fit in the four boxes has to be donated to a charity. Each box can contain twenty-seven books. What is the best estimate of the number of books Ella can pack?
Steps: Either use the compatible number (25 x 4) or round up (30 x 4)
Answer: Either 100 or 120, depending on whether you use compatible numbers or round.
Tips for Modifying: For an easier problem, give all numbers in standard number form. For a harder problem, use larger numbers. You could also complicate this by specifying that there are certain types of books (mysteries, sci-fi, fantasy, western, etc.) and that each has a different volume. A box has a given volume. The challenge then becomes determining how many of which kind she can take that would let her take the largest number of books.

150.
Difficulty: Easy
Skills Needed: rounding, division
Problem: Mary Krismiss is going to buy a bunch of toys for her Pomeranian for Christmas. She has $20 to use to buy dog toys. The toys cost $2.50 each. Using rounding or compatible numbers, what's the best estimate of the number of toys Mary can get?
Steps: $20 /$3 and drop the remainder or $21 / $3
Answer: 6 or 7, depending on whether you round or use compatible numbers.
Tips for Modifying: For an easier problem, use a number that is closer to an exact dollar amount. For a harder problem, use numbers that are less compatible or have a range the toys cost.

151.
Difficulty: Easy-Moderate
Skills Needed: adding, rounding
Problem: Ida Hoe's dog likes to eat dry dog food, but she's weird. She eats clusters of the little pellets. One day, she ate 3,392 pellets. The next day she ate 358 pellets. The third day, she ate 2,759 pellets. The fourth

day, she ate 8,529 pellets. The fifth day, she ate 2,859 pellets. To the nearest thousand, how many total pellets did she eat in the five days?
Steps: 3000 + 0 + 3000 + 9000 + 3000
Answer: 18,000
Tips for Modifying: For an easier problem, reduce the number of days or use significantly smaller numbers. For a harder problem, require some calculations for each day, like the dog eats some in the morning and some at night. Increase the number of days or use significantly large numbers.

152.
Difficulty: Easy-Moderate
Skills Needed: multiplication, rounding, days per week
Problem: Every day, Johnny B. Good's bird, Munchkin, eats his pellets. He eats exactly 3,728 pellets per day. Round that to the nearest thousand and find out approximately how much Munchkin eats by the end of the week.
Steps: 4000 x 7
Answer: 28,000 pellets
Tips for Modifying: For an easier problem, use significantly smaller numbers. For a harder problem, use significantly larger numbers or vary the number per day.

153.
Difficulty: Easy-Moderate
Skills Needed: multiplication, rounding, addition
Problem: Jerry Mander has 2 dogs. Dot eats 143 pellets every day. Spot, though, is so busy being silly, he only eats 78 pellets every day. After figuring out how many total pellets they eat in one day, round that to the nearest hundred. Then figure out how many total pellets they eat in 3 days and round to the nearest thousand.
Steps: (143 + 78) = 221; Round to 200. 200 x 3 = 600; Round to the nearest thousand.
Answer: 1000 pellets

Basic Math

Tips for Modifying: For an easier problem, use compatible numbers. For a harder problem, use larger numbers.

154.
Difficulty: Easy-Moderate
Skills Needed: finding range, addition, multiplication
Problem: Gene has four tomato plants. The puniest plant has four tomatoes on it. The most impressive plant has sixteen on it. Within what range will the total number of tomatoes fall?
Steps: Method 1: create a chart with 2 columns and 4 rows. On the top row of both columns put the smallest number of tomatoes. In the bottom row of both columns put the largest number of tomatoes. For the left column, fill in the blanks with the smallest number of tomatoes. For the right column fill in the blanks with the largest number of tomatoes. Add both columns.
Method 2: Multiply the smallest number by the number of plants. Multiply the biggest number by the number of plants.
Answer: Method 1: 28-52 tomatoes
Method 2: 16-64 tomatoes
Tips for Modifying: For an easier problem, use compatible numbers. For a harder problem, use larger numbers.

155.
Difficulty: Easy-Moderate
Skills Needed: rounding, adding, translating words to numbers
Problem: Betty Khan has a bunch of safety pins with beads on them. Each bead means something. She has four hundred fifty-two blue beads that mean "friendship." She has fifty-two red beads that mean "I don't like you." She has sixty-nine thousand pink beads that mean "love." She has fourteen green beads that mean "Go away already." To the nearest thousand, how many beads does she have?

Steps: 0 + 0 + 69,000 + 0 or 452 + 52 + 69,000 + 14
Round to the nearest 1000
Answer: 69,000 or 70,000 depending on whether you round before or after calculating
Tips for Modifying: For an easier problem, give all numbers in standard number form. For a harder problem, use significantly bigger numbers or increase the types of beads.

156.
Difficulty: Easy-Moderate
Skills Needed: rounding, addition, multiplication
Problem: Daisy is going to give her mom a big bunch of flowers. She bought 4 carnations for $.78 each and 10 roses for $2.23 each Round the money to the nearest dollar then find the best estimate of the amount of money Daisy spent.
Steps: ($1 x 4) + ($2 x 10)
Answer: $24
Tips for Modifying: For an easier problem, use more-compatible numbers. For a harder problem, make the amount of one flower the factor of the other such as three times as many roses as carnations. Add in additional flower types.

157.
Difficulty: Easy-Moderate
Skills Needed: estimation, multiplication
Problem: Avi Dreeder has 200 books in his collection. If each book cost him $6.99, about how much did he spend for all his books?
Steps: 200 x $7
Answer: $1400
Tips for Modifying: For an easier problem, use smaller numbers. For a harder problem, divide the books into categories (westerns, fantasies, sci-fi, histories, etc.), each of which cost a different amount.

Basic Math

158.
Difficulty: Moderate
Skills Needed: multiplication, recognizing "pair," addition, translating words to numbers
Problem: Eighteen pairs of bears of bears had 19 cubs in one year. If this continued every year for 5 years and none of the bears died, how many total bears would there be at the end of 5 years? After you find that answer, round to the nearest 10.
Steps: (2 x 18) + (19 x 5) Round to the tens.
Answer: 130 bears
Tips for Modifying: For an easier problem, give all numbers in standard number form or use compatible numbers. For a harder problem, set up a pattern so that each pair of bears produces some number of cubs. The cubs of one year join the breeding pairs for the next year.

159.
Difficulty: Moderate
Skills Needed: finding range, multiplication, inches per foot
Problem: June Ipper's dog jumps about three hundred times per hour. He jumps about 15-18 inches each time. If she adds all the distances he jumps, without rounding or using compatible numbers between jumps, what is the maximum and minimum number of feet he jumps in one hour?
Steps: (15" x 300 jumps) / 12"/ft
(18" x 300 jumps) / 12"/ft
Answer: 375' – 450'
Tips for Modifying: For an easier problem, use smaller or more-compatible numbers. For a harder problem, use larger numbers or give jumps per minute instead of hours but still require the answer in hours.

160.
Difficulty: Moderate
Skills Needed: rounding, division, translating words to numbers

Problem: Molly Cottle is buying fish for her fish tank. Each fish is seventy-five cents. She has ten dollars. If you round the money to the nearest dollar, approximately how many fish will she end up getting?
Steps: $10 / $1/fish
Answer: 10 fish
Tips for Modifying: For an easier problem, give numbers in standard number form or pick a cost for the fish that is closer to the dollar. For a harder problem, use less-compatible numbers.

161.
Difficulty: Moderate-Hard
Skills Needed: rounding, multiplication
Problem: Annie Malluver ran for the office of Chief Hamster Petter. If she wins, she gets to pet a hamster every day for 39 minutes. After rounding to the nearest half-hour, estimate how long would it take her to amass 15 hours of hamster petting time?
Steps: 1/2 hour is the nearest half hour for the petting time per day and there are 2 half-hours per hour so 15 x 2 is the days
Answer: 30 days.
Tips for Modifying: For an easier problem, use smaller or more-compatible numbers. For a harder problem, vary the amount of time for each day of the week.

Basic Math

Fractions

162.
Difficulty: Easy
Skills Needed: comparing fractions
Problem: Aaron Mitires and Cara Mehome got into a disagreement about which was larger ½ of a pizza or 5/10 of a pizza. Which one is bigger?
Steps: Use a drawing or the butterfly trick (multiply the numerator of one fraction by the denominator of the other fraction and put the product near the numerator you used. The largest product will be attached to the largest fraction) or any other handy strategy for figuring out which fraction is bigger.
Answer: They're the same fraction.
Tips for Modifying: For an easier problem, provide manipulatives. For a harder problem, add more fractions.

163.
Difficulty: Easy-Moderate
Skills Needed: multiplying by a fraction, rounding
Problem: Gravity on Earth = 1. Gravity on the moon = 1/6 of Earth. Wayan Tonn weighs 100 pounds on Earth. He calculated his weight on the moon as about 17 pounds. How did he do that calculation?
Steps: 100 x 1 / 6. Round the answer. Write out the process.
Answer: Multiply 100 by 1 then divide by 6. Round up.
Tips for Modifying: For an easier problem, make an alien world with an easier fraction of gravity, like one half. For a harder problem, make an alien world with a harder fraction for gravity like 2/5.

164.
Difficulty: Moderate
Skills Needed: the meaning of "dozen," subtraction, improper and mixed fractions, multiplication
Problem: Daisy made five batches of cookies when Miranda came over to play. Miranda and Daisy each ate

five cookies. If there are 2 dozen cookies in a batch, write a mixed fraction and an improper fraction to represent how many dozens of cookies left.
Steps: (2 dozen x 12 cookies/dozen x 5 batches) - (2 kids x 5 cookies/kid)
Convert to dozens
Answer: 9 2/12 dozens or 110/12 dozens
Tips for Modifying: For an easier problem, use smaller numbers. For a harder problem, use larger numbers or divide the cookies into types that have to be added together to get the total cookies.

165.
Difficulty: Moderate
Skills Needed: multiplying by a fraction
Problem: Rebecca broke a stick into sixty-two pieces. Each piece is ¾ inch long. How long was the original stick?
Steps: 62 pieces x 3/4"/piece
Answer: 46 1/2 inches
Tips for Modifying: For an easier problem, use a more compatible number or an easier fraction like 1/2. For a harder problem, use a larger number or vary the length of some pieces.

166.
Difficulty: Moderate
Skills Needed: multiplying by fractions, addition, subtraction
Problem: Kay Ick made a cake for the end of the year party. There were 60 pieces of the cake. The boys in the class ate 6/10 of the cake. The girls ate 2/5 of the cake. How many total pieces did the boys eat? How many total pieces did the girls eat? How many pieces are left?
Steps: 60 x 6 / 10 = boys
60 x 2 / 5 = girls
60 - (boys + girls)
Answer: Boys = 36, Girls = 24, Pieces left = 0
Tips for Modifying: For an easier problem, use easier fractions like halves or quarters. For a harder problem,

use less-compatible numbers or numbers that leave a remainder, so they have to figure out how to handle the remainder.

167.
Difficulty: Moderate
Skills Needed: equivalent fractions, translating words to numbers
Problem: Dot Yereyes is editing her friend's paper. For every four words of writing, she found a mistake. She found seventeen mistakes. Her friend found one mistake in Dot's paper for every ten words of writing. Dot's paper had ten mistakes. Who wrote the longest paper?
Steps: For Dot's friend, 1 word in 4 is wrong. There are 17 words wrong. Set that up as a ratio: 1/4 = 17/? To get from 1 to 17, you multiply by 17, so multiply 4 by 17 to get the denominator. The denominator is the length of the paper.
Likewise on Dot's paper. 1/10=10/? To get from 1 to 10, you multiply by 10, so multiply the denominator by 10. That gives you the length of that paper.
Answer: Dot wrote a longer paper.
Tips for Modifying: For an easier problem, use more-compatible numbers. For a harder problem, toss in a third writer or make the error rate more variable, such as 5 errors per 20 words in the first ten 100 words then 3 errors per ten words for the next 100 words.

168.
Difficulty: Moderate
Skills Needed: ratios or equivalent fractions, multiplication, division
Problem: Doc Sooned is teaching his dachshund Spike how to play fetch. Spike will return the ball 5 times out of 7. How many times must Doc throw the ball to get the ball back 50 times?
Steps: Start with 5/7. The numerator you need is 50. Find out how many times 5 divides into 50. Multiply that by the denominator 7.
Answer: 70 times

Tips for Modifying: For an easier problem, use smaller numbers. For a harder problem, use less-compatible numbers.

169.
Difficulty: Moderate-Hard
Skills Needed: dividing by fractions
Problem: Berry Pie's bird eats 2/5 of her mass every day in food. She eats 25 grams of food. What is her mass?
Steps: 25 x 5 / 2
Answer: 62.5 grams
Tips for Modifying: For an easier problem, use a more intuitive fraction like half. For a harder problem, divide the food up into types like vegetables, fruits, and seeds. Give each a mass.

170.
Difficulty: Hard
Skills Needed: converting time units, multiplication, division
Problem: Bob Ingduck, Al Umminim, and Tyya Knot are in a race to see who can put a list of words in alphabetical order the fastest. Bob can organize 5 words every fifteen seconds. Al can organize 10 words every forty seconds. Tyya can organize 250 words in 5 minutes. Who wins?
Steps: First, everyone needs to be converted to the same amount of time. Get everyone to 1 minute.
To get Bob to 1 minute, multiply his words by 4 (4 sets of 15 seconds = 1 minute). That gives him 20 words/min.
For Al, first divide his by 2 to get him to 20 seconds. That's 5 words/20seconds. Now multiply by 3 to get 15 words/min.
For Tyya, divide hers by 5. That gives you 50 words per minute.
The one with the biggest number of words per minute is the winner.
Answer: Tyya wins.
Tips for Modifying: For an easier problem, use more-

Basic Math

compatible numbers that are easier to convert to one minute. For a harder problem, add other people into the contest or use less-compatible numbers.

Acknowledgements

A hearty thanks to Kat Heckenbach and Victoria Adams for having a look at this book and offering suggestions on formatting and organization.

Previously published educational guides:

Finished? Now Get Busy (Kindle)

Writing Prompts for Intermediate Grades (Kindle)

Language Arts Centers for Intermediate Grades (Kindle)

Crunchy Word Problems & other Brain Challenges (Kindle)

Originally from Michigan, Cindy Koepp combined a love of pedagogy and ecology into a 14-year career as an elementary science specialist. After teaching four-footers (that's height, not leg count), she pursued a Master's in Adult Learning with a specialization in Performance Improvement. Her published works include science fiction and fantasy novels, a passel of short stories, and educator resources. When she isn't reading or writing, Cindy is currently working as a tech writer, hat collector, quilter, and crafter.